William Henry Sallmon

The Culture of Christian Manhood

Sunday mornings in Battell chapel, Yale university

William Henry Sallmon

The Culture of Christian Manhood
Sunday mornings in Battell chapel, Yale university

ISBN/EAN: 9783337369385

Printed in Europe, USA, Canada, Australia, Japan

Cover: Foto ©Lupo / pixelio.de

More available books at **www.hansebooks.com**

The Culture of Christian Manhood

Sunday Mornings
In Battell Chapel
Yale University ✠

Edited by
William H. Sallmon

With Portraits of Authors

"So full of grandeur is our dust,
So near is God to man,
When duty whispers low, 'Thou must,'
The youth replies, 'I can.'"
— EMERSON

NEW YORK   CHICAGO   TORONTO
Fleming H. Revell Company
M DCCC XCVII

Copyright, 1897, by
FLEMING H. REVELL COMPANY

THE NEW YORK TYPE-SETTING COMPANY

THE CAXTON PRESS

Contents

	PAGE
PREFACE	9
I. SELECTED LIVES	13
By Charles Cuthbert Hall, D.D.	
II. THE PART WE KNOW	30
By Alexander McKenzie, D.D.	
III. PERSONALITY	47
By Amory H. Bradford, D.D.	
IV. THE EVOLUTION OF A THINKER	63
By George A. Gordon, D.D.	
V. THE GREAT HERESY	81
By David James Burrell, D.D.	
VI. CHRIST SEEKING THE LOST	101
By George Harris, D.D.	
VII. AN EXTRAORDINARY SAINT	118
By William R. Richards, D.D.	
VIII. THE MEANING OF MANHOOD	138
By Henry van Dyke, D.D.	
IX. STRENGTH AND COURAGE	164
By Lewis O. Brastow, D.D.	

Contents

	PAGE
X. THE PERIL OF PROTRACTED TEMPTATION By Teunis S. Hamlin, D.D.	184
XI. THE GOSPEL'S VIEW OF OUR LIFE By Rev. Joseph H. Twichell	200
XII. TROPHIES OF YOUTH THE SAFEGUARD OF MANHOOD By Rev. James G. K. McClure	216
XIII. MANHOOD'S STRUGGLE AND VICTORY By S. E. Herrick, D.D.	233
XIV. THE SABBATH By Bishop John H. Vincent	249
XV. IMMUTABILITY By M. Woolsey Stryker, D.D., LL.D.	272
XVI. THE SINLESS ONE By George T. Purves, D.D.	286

PREFACE

WHEN that prince of American preachers, the late Bishop Brooks, after careful deliberation, declined to accept the call to the pulpit at Harvard University, he remarked to a friend that "the man who can preach helpfully to university men is the man who holds a city pastorate." The colleges are rapidly coming to this conclusion, and the college pastorate is giving way to the new system of college preachers. The pastoral work, where it is attended to at all, is cared for by other agencies. A few colleges, indeed, combine both methods, but in all the tendency is to place the main emphasis on the preaching. The preacher now comes in from the busy world toward which so many of the students are looking, and gives them glimpses

Preface

of it. He comes from contact with a broader life than a settled college pastor could be acquainted with, and he brings the prestige of an exalted position, and a greater enthusiasm for the large opportunity opened before him than could be maintained by a permanent resident. Naturally enough, the ablest men of the country are ready to respond to the call for such noble service. "No thinking minister can stand up before a company largely composed of young men without a strong wish to be plain-spoken and to come straight to the point. They have a fine impatience for all mere formalities and roundabout modes of speech, which acts as a moral tonic to brace the mind from vagueness and cleanse the tongue from cant. They want a man to say what he means and to mean what he says. The influence of this unspoken demand is wholesome and inspiring, and the preacher ought to show his gratitude for it by honestly endeavoring to meet it." These words, from one who occupies an influential city parish and commands the respect of col-

Preface

lege men wherever he meets them, will account for the direct and practical character of the discourses in this book. They have been selected for what they are worth in themselves, and will repay reading and re-reading. The editor takes pleasure in introducing some of the finest minds in the American pulpit,—with the messages of inspiration which they have brought to the members of Yale University,—hoping that the influence of their words will be multiplied many-fold by thus being put into permanent form.

Wm. N. Tallman

Selected Lives

By
Charles Cuthbert Hall, D.D.
President of the Union Theological Seminary, New York

" That ye may be . . . children of God . . . in the midst of a crooked and perverse generation, among whom ye are seen as lights in the world, holding forth the word of life."
—*Phil. ii. 15, 16.*

MY theme is *Selected Lives; or, the Distinction Conferred on Men by Academic Training.* Selected lives are lives singled out from the mass: set apart, trained, and commissioned unto a special opportunity. The basis of selection may be chiefly that of physical competency, as when men are selected for service in the army or in the athletic games. Or it may be chiefly that of intellectual culture, as in competitions for posts of honor in literary life. Or it may be chiefly that of spiritual efficiency, as when

Selected Lives

Christ selected apostles, saying, "Ye did not choose me, but I chose you, and appointed you, that ye should go and bear fruit, and that your fruit should abide." To-day my purpose is to remind you, as university men, that by reason of your being here, in the academic atmosphere, among the academic traditions, inheriting the academic privileges, you *are* selected lives singled out from the mass, set apart, trained, and commissioned unto a special opportunity. Standing in this great congregation of college men, I feel that I may speak without reserve of the distinction conferred on men by academic training. It is difficult to speak of this in a promiscuous assembly, where non-collegians are blended with collegians, lest one be thought to disparage the excellent and forceful men who have not had the university training; but in the pulpit of this venerable seat of learning, in an atmosphere charged with the purest and the best essence of the academic spirit, I feel no hesitation in reminding you that because you are collegians you constitute a class

The Individuality of Men

of selected lives; I feel no reserve in applying to you and in breathing upon you that glorious apostolic prayer for selected lives which is our text: "That ye may be children of God in the midst of a crooked and perverse generation, among whom ye are seen as lights in the world, holding forth the word of life."

If instead of the hundreds of men present this morning there were but one man, and he a man of thoughtful, noble spirit, it would be easy to deliver to him the message God has laid upon my heart. I would bid him ponder the thought of a selected life. I would bid him note *how* he has been selected, *why* he has been selected. I would bid him accept his destiny.

But while it would be easy to talk with one man alone of these things that lie so near to his personality, it is not difficult, because of the intense love and sympathy I feel toward young men, to speak to each one of you, in this hour, with a clear and impressive sense of your individuality. The message, then, is this: the selected life; the mode of its selection; the end of its selection; the acceptance of destiny.

First and chiefly, the Selected Life. I can conceive of nothing to which a noble soul responds more profoundly than to the sense of being a selected life: a life chosen, set apart, exalted from the mass, specialized unto a purpose. We have read to-day the splendid story of the anointing of David;* of the mystic purpose that singled him out from among his brethren, that called him from the sheepfold, that would not let his life grow narrow and rustic and indolent, basking in the sun on upland pastures, but drew it as with the cords of love unto a loftier, broader destiny, drew it to the leadership of men, setting it apart with the sacred oil of a royal anointing. It is a wondrous picture: that beautiful boy, whose life till now has been so pure, so natural, so simple, out upon the hills, where he has watched the white clouds sailing over him, where he has felt the free wind

* 1 Sam. xvi. 1-13.

The Royal Anointing

of God playing upon him, while his heart, unburdened by any care, has lived in the sunny present, giving, perchance, scarcely a thought to the future. But in the hour of his anointing it dawns upon him that he is a selected life—that he, yes, he! is set apart for an unusual destiny. What thought is greater than this to a soul that is noble? To feel the anointing of God upon itself; to know that it is called out from the mass, selected and set apart for something! It is an exalting thought—so high that often at the first one cannot attain unto it. While we all know that there are and ever have been selected lives, and while we all recognize selection in others who by their gifts and callings and opportunities are manifestly set apart in the world as its leaders, there is much difficulty for many a noble soul in conceiving of itself as one of the called. But when that thought comes home—when one is brought to feel that the anointing oil is upon one's own brow, and that life must henceforth have meanings reaching far beyond one's self and touching the destinies of others—the mind can hold few thoughts more exalting. A deep joy rises in the soul, "a tide too full for sound or foam," a sense of having caught some of Christ's meaning when he said, "I came that ye might have life, and that ye might have it more abundantly." Yet this exalting thought of being a selected life brings no pride, no shallow vanity to a noble soul, for it is also a most humbling thought. With the sense of one's own destiny comes a new conception of the broadness of life, and to know that God has anointed one for a purpose is also to realize the solemn meaning of living and the disproportion between one's powers and one's calling. The more sure we are that our lives have been selected from the mass for a purpose, the more conscious do we become of the deficiencies in ourselves that threaten to hinder, if not to prevent, the fulfilment of our calling. And thus the exalting thought, which is so truly the humbling thought, becomes also the sanctifying thought. The man on whom is dawning the conception

The Academic Brotherhood

of his own life as a selected life begins to feel the sacredness of living. He sees that he is not his own, that he is chosen and ordained for special duty in the kingdom of God, for special service in the world of men. And the spirit of consecration enters into his life —the desire to accept his destiny and to be made worthy of it.

Why do I place all this so earnestly before you to-day? Because I regard you as a body of selected lives. The fact that you are here, in the university circle, in the academic brotherhood, constitutes you members of a selected class in the world. Academic training confers a distinction upon men, sets them apart from the mass, specializes their opportunity, pours upon their foreheads the drops of a holy anointing. To claim this distinction for college men is to claim no more than facts will justify. Because you are members of a great and populous university, because you are accustomed to congregate as a small army among yourselves, because those of us who deal much with college problems are impressed with the growth and expansion of student life in this country, we are all likely to overestimate the proportion of college men in the population of the United States. But it can be shown by most carefully prepared statistics how relatively small is the student class, and how, for every young man entering the academic circle, hundreds must be denied the exalted privileges of that noble circle, save as we who have had those privileges, and have by means of them become a selected class, shall know the meaning of God's anointing upon ourselves, and shall go forth as lights in the world, holding forth the word of life to those who have not been called with our calling.

One difficulty stands in the way of your realizing that you are all—every one of you—selected lives, anointed and set apart for special influence in the world. That difficulty is the fact that *within* the university are such marked differences not only in the capacity of men to be leaders, but in the disposition of men to live nobly. There must be striking

Diversities of Gifts

differences of capacity among you. Doubtless you have natural leaders among you: men of brilliant personality and singular forcefulness, who come to the front in your counsels and achievements by a kind of natural and involuntary selection; men who would probably have been leaders anywhere, out of college or in college. And there can be no doubt that many a quieter man, many a man less richly endowed with the fascinating gifts of personality, is often depressed as he measures his own lesser influence against these born leaders, judging them to be selected to a class from which he has been left out. But the thought I am presenting to-day is larger than that which takes note of the scaling of personal gifts. It is a thought that includes every man among you in the class of selected lives, on whom God has poured a holy anointing. Your academic life is your anointing. You are selected because you are here, and because of what you should be made by being here. In every grouping of men there will be gradings of power—some men more

Selected Lives

evidently born for leadership than others. Even among the twelve apostles there were gradings of power and a few natural leaders. Yet all were called and selected and set apart by Christ to go out into the world and to spread the light of his coming up and down the world. And you, whatever the gradings of power among you, are *all* called, even from the least to the greatest, to go out into the mass of the world from which you have been singled and set apart, that you may be children of God in the midst of a crooked and perverse generation, among whom you are seen as lights in the world, holding forth the word of life. And the same is true in regard to the different dispositions which may be found among you toward living nobly. Your capacities may differ, while yet you are all called and selected; so also your moral dispositions may differ, while yet you are all called and selected, from the noblest to the most ignoble. There must be earnest men here, brave with a most exalted purpose, conscious that God has selected and anointed

Why were We Selected?

them for great ends. And there may be men here far less earnest, devoid of the spirit of consecration, idle, irresolute, yes, loving darkness rather than light. Yet *they* are selected lives and anointed lives as much as the others, by virtue of their being in this academic brotherhood; and the carelessness of their lives is a more serious and melancholy perversion of good because it is the denial of God's anointing and the misuse of *special* privilege. By the rule Christ himself laid down—" To whom much is given, of him shall much be required "—it is more grievous for a college man to live ignobly than for another, for his is the greater light, his the higher calling, his the more royal anointing.

But how came this selection, my brothers, to be set on us? How is it *we* are here, while others whom we have known are not here and can never be here? How were we singled out and selected to live within this academic circle, closed against hundreds of our contemporaries? Ah, that is a deep question; deep and far-reaching must be its answer. Doubtless many of us are here through the consecrated self-denial of others on our behalf. There are those who love us, who think they see in us signs of God's selecting grace, who have borne and are bearing mighty burdens, that we through their poverty might be made rich with the intellectual and spiritual wealth of the academic life. I know the fathers who are practising heroic self-privation, some of them in remote and ill-paid pastorates, that their sons may enter manhood within this circle of selected lives. I know the young sister who is hoarding her scant income as a teacher, that her younger brother may not lack the privilege of a European university. Doubtless many of us are here through the mystic influence of heredity. The strain of intellectual tendency is in our blood, an ancestral heritage. We were projected into this circle by the momentum of an intellectual predestination, gathering force, it may be, from colonial times. Our selection was prenatal. We are what we are because our fathers and their

For what are We Selected?

fathers were what they were. And doubtless many of us are here through the direct and obvious calling of the Spirit of God. I doubt whether Christ's selection of his apostles was more emphatic or more individualistic than his call and selection of some of us to come into this circle, and live his life, and follow in his train, and go out into our generation and be seen in it as lights in the world, holding forth the word of life. Can any one of us entertain the belief that he is here because of Christ's choosing, and not offer up his very life to Christ in full response, saying, with Johann Scheffler:

> "O Love, who ere life's earliest dawn
> On me thy choice hast gently laid;
> O Love, who here as Man wast born,
> And wholly like to us wast made;
> O Love, I give myself to thee,
> Thine ever, only thine, to be."

And unto what are we selected? What is the end and object of the distinction conferred on men by their academic training? It is— to speak the apostolic word with direct reference to the national and social and spiritual questions of our own country and of our own time—it is that we may stand in the midst of our crooked and perverse generation, our generation which has so many distorted ideas and unwholesome practices, and be as lights in the world, holding forth the word of life. It is that we may show in ourselves and promote in others nobler citizenship, politically, socially, spiritually. It was many years ago that Benson, the fine-spirited Archbishop of Canterbury, who died so suddenly at Hawarden, said, in his impassioned way, to the boys at Wellington College: "As citizens men despise their birthr'ghts." We have been compelled to witness much of that despising of the civic birthright on this side of the sea; much of a corrupt citizenship, selling its birthright for money, estimating the public service by its gains. God forbid that I should seem to imply that the line dividing the noble from the ignoble in the ethics of citizenship is the collegiate education; that the citizens who honor their birthright are not numerously found among those who never matriculated in college. Patriotism in its purest form may be found in every social order of our land. But I do affirm the peculiarly great opportunities given to him who combines with a pure spirit a liberal education, to become a light in the world, a leader of his countrymen toward higher and broader conceptions of national honor and of civic duty. The college man in politics is the salvation of the present and the hope of the future. Training tells. The untrained mind may be as lofty in its intention as the mind of a scholar. But the academic discipline joined with the academic point of view are indispensable for statesmanship; and what this country chiefly needs is a race of statesmen, *selected lives*, trained in the university to estimate upon the historic basis the trend of events, nurtured in the university upon the ideals of a fervent, white-souled patriotism, kindled in the university with that sublime ambition to serve the state for the state's sake which makes citizenship a high profession and the birthright within the nation a holy and unsullied trust. It is a great thing to go forth as a collegian into the vast territory of philanthropic, moral, and Christian opportunity. It is a great thing to be a collegian in these latter days, and to have part in this mighty expansion of sociology as a practical science. It is a great thing to be a collegian and to carry the skill and fire of an academic training into the moral movement of our day. It is a great thing to be a collegian in these times, and in the holy ministry of Jesus to go out and preach a simple Christianity, a more fraternal and catholic churchmanship, a gospel whose spirit is first of all and above all the missionary spirit.

Selected lives, called by the Spirit and the providence of God into peculiar privilege and specialized opportunity, accept your destiny. It is within your grasp, to have and to hold, or to reject and to throw away. God puts your opportunity into your hand. If you use it your life will be a victory; if you put it from you some other man will gladly seize it and conquer where you failed. May

Our Opportunity

I not in this place speak—not into your ears only, into your very hearts—the message of a Yale man of the class of '61, Edward Rowland Sill? It is his wonderful parable of opportunity, a parable for each selected life to ponder: of the coward who flung away his sword upon a vain excuse, and of the king's son, he on whose brow were the drops of the royal anointing, who seized the sword the coward flung away and with it won a splendid triumph for the cause of truth:

" This I beheld—or dreamed it in a dream:
There spread a cloud of dust along a plain;
And underneath the cloud, or in it, raged
A furious battle, and men yelled, and swords
Shocked upon swords and shields. A prince's banner
Wavered, then staggered backward, hemmed by foes.
A craven hung along the battle's edge,
And thought: ' Had I a sword of keener steel,—
That blue blade that the king's son bears,—but this
Blunt thing!—' he snapt and flung it from his hand,
And lowering crept away and left the field.
Then came the king's son, wounded, sore bestead,
And weaponless, and saw the broken sword,
Hilt-buried in the dry and trodden sand,
And ran and snatched it, and, with battle-shout
Lifted afresh, he hewed his enemy down
And saved a great cause that heroic day."

The Part We Know

By

Alexander McKenzie, D.D.
Minister of the First Church in Cambridge

"Silver and gold have I none; but such as I have give I thee."—Acts iii. 6.

THESE are very simple words. The thought is neither original nor profound, but it has always been a popular verse. Perhaps this is because we are so often asked to give what we cannot give, or we require ourselves to do what we cannot do, that there is special encouragement in being told on high authority that we can only do what we can and give what we have.

The incident itself is familiar. A man lame from his birth was laid at the Beautiful Gate of the Temple at the time of the evening worship. He saw the two Galileans,

The Value of Money

Peter and John, entering in, and he looked to them for an alms. They fastened their eyes upon his longing eyes, and Peter said, "Silver and gold have I none." It was silver and gold the man wanted, and his rising hope fell into disappointment. But Peter finished his sentence, "Such as I have give I thee," and the man was content. The first words are of little account, save as a natural beginning. The latter words hold the force of the sentence. It was of no consequence to Peter or to the man what the apostle had not; the strength was entirely on the positive side. "What I have" is in itself a strong sentence. Happily, that which he had was in itself of much greater value than that which he lacked. Silver and gold are of great worth, but they cannot do all things. They can build a hospital, but they cannot create physicians. They can endow a college, but they cannot make scholars. When we call the physician to our necessity we do not care whether he has silver and gold or not, and men have been eminent as college professors who were in no wise distinguished by their wealth. Indeed, the need of silver and gold may be a stimulus to exertion, as when the great English lawyer sprang suddenly into his first great cause and great fame, and assigned as the reason for his remarkable effort that he felt his children pulling at his gown and crying, "Father, give us bread." On the other hand, the possession of wealth may lessen the exertion. When Thomas Aquinas visited Innocent IV., the pope displayed the great treasures of the church and boasted, "The time has gone by when the church must say, 'Silver and gold have I none.'" "Yes," was the answer of the saintly doctor, "and the time has gone by when the church can say to a lame man, 'Rise up and walk.'" The wise man knows the use of wealth, while he keeps himself independent of it. It was a fine assertion of independence made by the English prelate at New Zealand, when the authorities in England warned him that if he persisted in his course they should cut down his salary. "You can get very good fish here in the

Variety in Helpfulness

bay," he said, "and I know a place in the woods where you can dig up roots that you can eat." What could be more absurd than the attempt to control through his salary the utterances of a man who can live on roots!

But if we are not to have silver and gold, let us by all means have something. There is so great variety in the wants of men that there is great variety in the help which can be given to them. Think how many things might have been done for this lame man. He could have been furnished with money; he could have been furnished with sound feet and ankle-bones; one who could have done nothing more might have moved him into a comfortable position against the wall, or have drawn his rug over his feet, or brought him a piece of bread or a cup of water. But the man in his want represents the world and its necessities, and suggests the varied opportunities calling for whatever endowment of skill or strength one may possess. Peter was able to give to him the best gift when with the divine power intrusted to him he lifted

The Part We Know

up a man who had never stood upon his feet and gave him strength to take up the work of life and to walk in its pleasant places. This was Peter's grace. It may not be yours or mine, but it is given to every one of us to have something which the world needs and which we can give as the manifesting of our life. Let us make sure, by all means, that we have something which the world needs, and that we are using what we have, not hindered by what we lack. Negative lives are of small value. Negative acts, if there are such things, are not worthy of men in the serious work of life. The phrase sometimes used of an act which we like to perform, that "there is no harm in it," is not worthy of a man. It is not what an act does not have in it, but what an act does have in it, that should enlist our care. An act with no harm in it is a purse with no money in it; it is not equal to the needs of our daily life, while we are easily able to have money in our purse. The requirements of God do not stop at the negatives. "Do not covet" means "Love." "Do

The Positive Life

not lie" means "Tell the truth." "Do not steal" means "Give." For our own sake and for the world's sake let us keep on this side of possession and accomplishment. A colorless life is of no honor and no use. To commend a man for having no fault is often to reproach a man for having no virtue. Stand for something; have a place and be a force in the world. They asked John the Baptist who he was. He made little account of what he was not, and we are not impressed by his words, "I am not the Christ. I am not that prophet." It is the positive side of his declaration which marks the man and asserts his force: "I am the voice." The two great confessions in the midst of the gospel are confessions upon the positive side: "Thou art the Christ, the Son of the living God." "Thou art Peter, and on this rock will I build my church." Stand for something. There is an expression of great strength used by St. Paul in writing to the Corinthian church: "Ye are members in particular"; not "members," not "members in general," not "members upon the catalogue," but members with a definite place and work and honor and reward—"members in particular." I am walking with you, and I point to a man whom we see upon the street, and I say, "Who is that man?" You answer, "He is nobody in particular." "But he is a man, is he not?" "Oh yes; he lives here; I meet him frequently; you will find his name in the city directory. But that is all; he is nobody in particular." Another day we meet another man, perhaps more plainly dressed, more simple in his bearing, and I repeat my question, "Who is that man?" "That man? Why, that is the finest lawyer in the town. That man was governor of the commonwealth. That man is the leading professor in the college." "Ah, I see; you have not told me his name, but you have told me the man. He is what St. Paul meant; he is somebody 'in particular.'"

A positive life is the life of the highest accomplishment and is lived in the highest domain. There are many things that we do

Knowledge More than Ignorance

not know. There is a part of everything that we do not know. We are all undergraduates in the university of life. But we know in part; that is, in part we know. So St. Paul teaches us. Use that part. What we do not know is of little practical value compared with the part that we do know. If I may adapt the saying, our knowledge, however small, is of greater account than our ignorance, however great. We should be very glad that it is only a part that we know. Life would be dismal indeed if we had reached the limit of truth upon any of its broad lines; if there were no more great verities than we have compassed or can soon compass; if duty and truth and life were all held within our slender grasp; if there were no more of glory and honor and immortality than we can see and understand and value and make our own. It is the almost limitless extent of truth which makes it divine, and the endless years that are awaiting us are to be filled with the endless attainment of knowledge and grace and life. St. Paul, with all his visions of eternal

The Part We Know

grace and life, rejoiced to confess, reveled in the confession, that that in which he was living passed his knowledge. So St. John, rising to his sublime conception of the character of the saints, poured out his exultant heart in the great confession, "Beloved, now are we the sons of God, and it doth not yet appear what we shall be." But while they knew in part they used the part they knew; they rested their own life upon it; they gave it to others for their learning; they breathed it upon the world for its inspiration; they believed in the steadily rising sun and the day that eternally shall grow brighter and brighter. It is little to say that our knowledge, too, is in part. Our knowledge of God is very far from perfect. We believe in God, the Father Almighty. We know the love of God. We rejoice in his providence. But no man hath seen God at any time, nor can see him. Yet upon this knowledge of God which we do possess we build a life of confidence, obedience, affection, the strong life of a child of God to whom there comes the continual

The Obedience of Our Verities

growth in all that is godly and divine in the power of an endless life. We know Jesus Christ, our Lord and Saviour. We know that the eternal Word was made flesh and has dwelt among us. We know that life of divine beauty and help. We know the parables of truth and the miracles of mercy, and that he loved the world and gave himself for it, the Lamb of God, the Saviour of men, forevermore Redeemer and Intercessor. But the method of the incarnation we do not know. The full secret of redemption we cannot trace. The secret working of the Holy Ghost in the souls of men we cannot define. Yet we open our hearts to the Comforter; we intrust ourselves to the Redeemer; we follow him who is the light and the life of men. We know in part, but the part we know is the part we use. To use the part we know is to know more. Not the fondling of our doubts, but the obedience of our verities leads up the heights of knowledge.

Perhaps there is no better illustration of the method of life which is here commended

The Part We Know

than that which is given in the gospel in the case of the man who was born blind. His ignorance was very great and his knowledge was very small. Christ came that way, and spoke to him, and bade him go wash in the pool of Siloam. The man heard the voice, understood the direction, went down the hill, and in that very act made the beginning of a Christian life, for he had done at Christ's word, though he had never seen Christ, what no one else had ever done, what he had never dreamed of doing, what no other one would ever have asked him to do. He knew that he was told to go and wash in Siloam, and he went. He came back seeing, and his trouble began. His life had been an easy one, narrow, dull, but free from great anxiety or large exertion. From that time men who should have rejoiced in the gift which came to him gathered around him to annoy him and accuse him, to make his new sight a burden to him; and even his father and mother, to whom he might have looked for sympathy, turned upon him the hard faces which seemed to make it

The Wise Blind Man

hardly worth the while to be able to look upon the features of a friend. The poor man's ignorance was appalling, but shrewdly he took hold of what he knew and worked simply with that. "This man is a sinner," people said to him. They denounced, and they would have him denounce, the stranger who had given him his sight. To all their reasoning he could make no answer. He was wise in keeping himself free from what he did not know. And finally, when they had worried and badgered him to the last, he cried out with the wit and shrewdness of a man who had done much thinking, with a poor appeal to pity in this confusion of his new gift; still clinging to the part he knew, he cried out in this wise: "Gentlemen, have compassion upon me. I am a poor man. I have never had any chance. I have never been to school. I cannot answer you. I do not know anything about these things you are throwing at me. Whether he be a sinner or no I know not. One thing I know: that, whereas I was blind, now I see." On that

The Part We Know

"pin-point of his experience" he stood, and from it nothing could move him. Well, they turned him out of the church. So much they could do. But they could not turn him out of himself or away from Christ. Jesus met him, for he heard that they had cast him out, and he turned a compassionate look upon the new eyes and said, "Dost thou believe on the Son of God?" Mark the answer. "If I knew who he was, I think I should believe on him"—it was not that he said. It was a forward, straight-out confession: "Who is he, Lord, that I might believe on him?" "Thou hast both seen him, and he it is that speaketh with thee." And he said, "Lord, I believe," and he worshiped him. Thus from the first moment when Jesus spoke to him to this last moment of revelation the man born blind stood in front of his ignorance, took what he knew, used what he knew, worked what he knew into his life, and became the confessor, the first man to suffer for his faith in Jesus Christ. What wonder that one of our most brilliant, philosophic preachers should say, "When I would know just what Christianity is in its last analysis I must make a careful study of what passed between Jesus and the man born blind"?

The times that we are living in greatly need this practical method. It is a day of negation. Great questions of religion and of life are under discussion. Nothing escapes the scrutiny of the eager, restless mind of man. Out of this time of removal the great truths will come, and they will not suffer shock. Meantime it is a period of unrest, and with many a period of increased uncertainty. With the best intentions, they feel less assured concerning many matters of faith which they have held of great account. But study cannot be checked, searching cannot be repressed, and we must wait in faith and patience, in the quiet confidence that the things which cannot and ought not to be shaken will remain. But for ourselves, for our personal life, for our influence in the world, the only manly rule is that which is suggested to us here by the blind man and by the apostle—

The Part We Know

to use what we have, and in the faithful employment of what we know to gain the steady accession of knowledge, the constant increase of its truth and power. If it be necessary to write over many a page "Silver and gold have I none," we certainly are able to write over many another page "Such as I have." This is the time for using what we have, and this is the place. The life in a university is too young to be mortgaged to ignorance. With the face set forward, with willing ears waiting for the call of duty, we are to be assured that it is a positive living which is called for, the use of what is in hand. It is in this way that all advance in study is made. We go from the alphabet that we know into the literature that stretches its endless reach beyond us. We go from the few figures learned in childhood to the high reckonings which mark the courses of the planets. Let it be so in all study: from what we have on to the greater having. In the use of what we have let us come to be Christ's disciples. In the use of what we

The Best Gift

have let us advance to higher discipleship, ever learning, ever teaching, steadily getting, steadily giving. When we take account of life let us give especial heed to that which we have. If we find that we have not the means by which we might do some work which is waiting for us, the result is not to be inactivity, but the doing some other work with the force in our hands. If we had silver and gold we would give them, but oftentimes they cannot meet the want, and oftentimes they are poor gifts. Modern charity has learned the lesson, and is striving to teach it to us, that money is seldom the best gift to the poor, but the help to get money, which shall maintain self-respect, promote industry and all the virtues. If, some day, I find I have no silver and gold, then let me go down to the Beautiful Gate of the Temple and work some simple miracle. I can help some lame man; I can read to some blind man; I can comfort and strengthen; I can bless; and even wanting many things which might be of service, I can do those larger things which

The Part We Know

Christ has told me of, saying, "The works that I do shall ye do; and greater works than these." Let us not forget that this incident at the Temple was but the picture of his life. Silver and gold Christ had none. In not one instance in the gospel did he give this kind of help, but he gave men strength and comfort and eternal life. One thing he always had, and he gave that. That one thing every man has, and, whatever be his property, every man, like Christ, can give—himself. And no man is poor who has himself to give.

Now let us away! Let us raise the sails. There is not much wind. But let us set the sails and get the anchors up on deck. There will be a strong breeze at night, and before morning we shall be well out to sea.

Personality

By

Amory H. Bradford, D.D.
Pastor of the First Congregational Church of Montclair, N. J.

"But lighting upon a place where two seas met, they ran the vessel aground."—Acts xxvii. 41.

WHO can describe a shipwreck?—fury of waves, terror of people, howling of winds, and roaring of waters! For fourteen days this ship on which the Roman centurion and his prisoners had taken passage was driven by the wind; for fourteen days there was sight neither of sun nor of stars. Two hundred and seventy-six persons were on board. Strength and courage were alike exhausted. There was no cessation of the storm. The sailors imagined that they were drawing near to land, and, sounding, found first a depth of twenty fathoms, then fifteen

Personality

fathoms; then, fearing lest they should be cast on a rocky shore, they put out four anchors from the stern. That method of anchoring ships was not uncommon in those times. They "wished for the day." How much is packed into those words! But there was selfishness even there. The sailors, professing to look after the anchors, lowered one of the ship's boats and were about to try to save themselves when they were exposed by Paul. As day began to dawn he moved among the people and begged them to take food, assuring them that they should all be saved. Not until he took the bread himself and calmly gave thanks to God were they willing to eat. A ship is comparatively safe in the open sea, even if the waves are piled into mountains; but when land is approached breakers make quick work of the strongest craft. In the dawning light they saw not far distant a bay, which they tried to reach. Having thrown overboard the wheat with which the ship was loaded, they cut loose the anchors, raised the sail, and made for the

Paul and the Shipwreck

haven. Suddenly they came to a place where two seas met. Then nothing remained but to run the vessel aground. The soldiers had to answer for their charge with their lives. Therefore they advised the centurion to kill the prisoners so that none should escape. He would not consent; thereupon both prisoners and passengers threw themselves into the waters, and all reached land.

We have seen Paul facing angry mobs; going alone through the mountains of Asia; in the presence of mocking philosophers in Corinth and Athens; before the Roman governor and the Jewish king; but we have never seen him in circumstances so trying as these. During weeks of storm he was the good angel of the ship. He cheered the sailors, comforted the prisoners, encouraged the centurion. When others expected to go to the bottom he was confident that all would be saved. Tradition represents him as of inferior presence—possibly of limping gait, very likely with some serious affection of his eyes, mean, as he has himself told us, in bodily

Personality

appearance. His power was in his qualities of spirit, and those he never more superbly manifested than when a prisoner on his way to the imperial city. The greatness of personality has seldom had a finer illustration than in his conduct in the midst of the shipwreck.

What do we mean by personality? It is all that distinguishes a man from a thing. When one is richly endowed in mind, heart, and will he has a strong personality. When the heart predominates over the intellect he has a sympathetic personality. When ambition prevails there is a malign personality. The word needs little definition; its meaning is evident. It may be a blessing or a curse. If it is used in the interests of love it is a blessing; if in the interests of selfishness it is a curse. Paul was an eager, impassioned, persistent enthusiast, a man of great intellect, inspired and fired with fervent love. His influence was the result of what he was. Personality is the sum of all the powers. Pascal, in one of his immortal "Pensées," has finely

Types of Heroism

said: "But were the universe to crush him, man would still be more noble than that which kills him, because he knows that he dies, and the universe knows nothing of the advantage it has over him." In other words, spirit is mightier than matter, and personality is always spiritual. Will can never be conquered by force. A child may defy a storm; the ocean may engulf the man whom it cannot destroy. I have never tired reading of the attempts of the late Professor Tyndall to scale the Matterhorn. He would not be prevented from planting his feet upon its loftiest peak and gazing upon the frozen ocean that broke into billows of snow and ice at its base. But personality is not so impressive when it is pitted against nature as when in a good man, alone and undaunted, it faces a throng who are strong and bad. The power one man may have over a multitude is vividly illustrated in the story of that monk who, hearing of the gladiatorial exhibitions in Rome, made his way to the imperial city and the Colosseum; and who,

Personality

as the brutal sport was about to begin, leaped from tier to tier of the crowded seats into the arena. Standing before the gladiators with drawn swords, he cried to the spectators in a voice which rang through all the arches: "Will you praise God by the shedding of innocent blood?" The spectacle did not cease that day, and he who tried to stop it was run through by the swords of the gladiators, but not until he had given a death blow to the barbarism that had long disgraced the so-called Christian empire.

> "His dream became a deed that woke the world,
> For while the frantic rabble in half-amaze
> Stared at him dead, thro' all the nobler hearts
> In that vast Oval ran a shudder of shame.
> The Baths, the Forum gabbled of his death,
> And preachers linger'd o'er his dying words,
> Which would not die, but echo'd on to reach
> Honorius, till he heard them, and decreed
> That Rome no more should wallow in this old lust
> Of Paganism, and make her festal hour
> Dark with the blood of man who murder'd man."

What most attracts toward higher ideals? The splendid utterances of orators? The finished sentences of brilliant authors? Our Master showed finer discernment when he sent

The Power of Character

his disciples into the world to do just as he had done. He attracted others by the evident goodness of his life—by the power of his personality. When he called, Peter and John left their nets and followed him. By the same methods his work is to be continued. Influence is not measured by words, but by character. No book was ever so well worth studying as a noble life. Men, not books, have lifted the world toward higher things. Some persons are so genuine, so true, so trustworthy, that in the hour of need they are always sought. The greatest figure in English history is that of Oliver Cromwell. But Cromwell did not leap into publicity at a bound. He was a country squire, in appearance uncouth, in manner without polish, with no gift of oratory; but he could be counted on. The times demanded "a still, strong man," who could "rule and dare not lie," and he was that man. What made Abraham Lincoln the idol of the republic and the glory of his generation? Not his eloquence, although few have spoken more eloquently;

Personality

not his achievements, although few have achieved greater things. He is remembered and loved for what he was. The little girl who pleaded for her brother found the great President's ear attentive; the widow with the story of her only boy found his heart sympathetic. He never ceased to be a man, and in that fact was his power. Culture alone is not personality; neither are wealth, a beautiful presence, an honored lineage, nor physical strength. "A little child shall lead them." We bow before strength, but that will fail; we admire intellect, but intellect is not always to be trusted. Show me one who will never deceive, who is honest as the day, unselfish as love, who never seeks his own but always another's welfare, and I will show you a man whom all who know will trust, before whom many hearts will open, and into whose keeping sacred secrets will be committed. The greatest power in the world is personal, and personal power culminates when wisdom and knowledge are married to goodness and

The Secret of Personality

love. When we are what we ought to *be* the things which we ought to *do* will be evident, and the strength to do them at hand.

If Paul was remarkable neither for physical strength nor for learning, and least of all for grace and charm of manner, then what was the secret of his unique personality? He would not have been long in answering that question. "The love of Christ constraineth me." By that he would mean, "The secret of my life is in the fact that the very love which was in Christ has reached down and taken hold of me and made me its glad and grateful slave." "Christ liveth in me." "I am crucified with Christ." The old Saul had gone out of sight, and a new man had come in, who was impelled by the very forces which took Jesus to the cross. The secret of his power, service, and endurance was in "the heavenly vision." Another element in Paul's personality was his large and vital faith. That is not synonymous with belief. Faith in a person is never the same as belief in a proposition. Faith is not the acceptance of a series of doctrines; it is the bond which links us with the unseen; it is the bridge which we throw over the abyss between ourselves and the infinite. "I believe in God so that I trust him" is a true description of faith.

Faith is the faculty of realizing in our mortal life the unseen and eternal, and love is the substitution of Christ's motives and methods for those of the world. These two graces combined in one character go far toward the making of an inspiring personality. Those who have "endured as seeing Him who is invisible," who have dared to face a majority in the consciousness of being right, who have followed love even though it has taken them to the cross, have been leaders to whom the world has come at last. That monument on Commonwealth Avenue in Boston is typical. There was a time when the most maligned man in America was William Lloyd Garrison. Even Boston was ready to hang him, for no reason except that he believed in God and loved man. He was

Faith and Love

not great, except in his passion for humanity. He would not sacrifice a brother to win a world's applause. The secret of heroism is always found in faith and love. No one is heroic without them. Those who trust God seldom fear man, and will not doubt that in the end truth and righteousness will prevail. If they go down beneath the waters it will be with a song upon their lips. He who forgets himself and lives for others, though he be as humble as the Galilean, will sooner or later inspire many with a passion for his ideal.

Four characteristics are always found in those who exert an enduring and beneficent influence. The first is devotion to God. Where there is no vision of God the tendency is ever and inevitably downward. Those who believe in no mountain-crests will seek to climb none. Those who have stooped lowest in service have previously been lifted highest by their beliefs. Those who have been surest of God and most consecrated to him have had the most faith in man and done the most for his elevation. Those who have visions of God sooner or later become like him. They are not attracted by evil, because they have fallen in love with the good. No one has led the race far toward the heavenly heights who has not been sure of God. All are heroic who can say, "Though he slay me, yet will I trust him."

The highest manhood necessitates the finest culture of mind and heart. An ignorant good man is never so efficient as one who has ample knowledge and has cultivated his faculties. Goodness is sometimes allied to coarseness, and culture to crime; circumstances often make culture impossible; but in themselves knowledge and training are elements of strength, and, other things being equal, he who knows much and who has been carefully trained will do most for God and man. All men are "loaded with bias." Something which will develop the good and make "a balance in the faculties" is desirable. God gives his Spirit to those who can use it best. Some ignorant men have done great

The Necessity of Purity

things, and some learned men have been fools; but no man ever accomplished much because he knew little, and no man was ever a fool because he was learned. Paul spent three years in Arabia before he began to preach. All teachers of abiding influence have spent more time in studying than in teaching. Every grace of manner, every gain of education, every charm of presence, every refinement of expression, will be sought by those who are anxious to achieve worthy things for the kingdom of God.

If personality and power are synonymous, then those habits which hinder the fullest and most beautiful development of the spirit should be put away. Fineness of spirit can manifest itself only through purity of body. All ought sometime to offer Tennyson's prayer:

> "Oh for a man to arise in me,
> That the man I am may cease to be."

Whatever dulls the intellectual faculties or dims the spiritual perception limits influence. Those who have found nearness to God have

Personality

begun by abstinence from all that pampers the flesh. Prophets have never spent much time in parlors. Gluttony and spirituality are sworn enemies. Narcotics and stimulants do not clarify spiritual sight. The pure in heart see God. The astronomer makes sure that the glass of his telescope is not soiled by a single fleck. The reflector in the lighthouse must be kept untarnished. If we would know God and thus be of some little service in making him known to our fellow-men, we must make sure that our thoughts are pure and our habits clean.

But perhaps the chief factor in a beneficent personality is loss of self in devotion to humanity. Sooner or later others will seek the man who never schemes for himself. Those who exalt themselves no one else will exalt. A physician, at the peril of his life, allowed a tube to be inserted into his veins, that blood might be drawn from him to save the life of a servant. Those who will risk their lives for the lowliest are made of heroic stuff. For such this world is waiting. Self-

The Prerogative of No Class

assertion is hateful; self-sacrifice to save one's fellow-men, sublime. The inscription on the tomb of General Gordon in St. Paul's Cathedral closes as follows: "Who at all times and everywhere gave his strength to the weak, his substance to the poor, his sympathy to the suffering, and his heart to God." No wonder that Chinamen listened to him as if he were a messenger from another world! No wonder that African tribes believed that he was a superior being! All who forget themselves in the service of God and man help to make grand, sweet music in the midst of the storm and shipwreck of this mortal life.

Personality is the prerogative of no class. The loftiest spirit may inhabit the frailest body and the whitest soul dwell in the deepest poverty. All who trust God and in the spirit of Christ serve their fellow-men enter into the secret places of abiding power. Devotion to the divine, the culture of every gift and faculty, body and mind "according well" and kept pure and clean, loss of self in

Personality

the consciousness of the privilege of serving humanity—these are the characteristics of that lofty and beneficent manhood so finely designated in our time by the word "personality," and perfectly illustrated for all time in the example of Him who came not to be ministered unto but to minister, and who by losing His life became the Saviour of the world.

The Evolution of a Thinker

By

George A. Gordon, D.D.
Pastor of the Old South Church, Boston, Mass.

*"I thought on my ways,
And turned my feet unto thy testimonies."*
Ps. cxix. 59.

THE thinker is always an interesting being; but sometimes he is a sophist, and, although interesting, he is misleading. And even when he is not a sophist he is frequently abstract, remote, vague, and therefore unprofitable. Here in the text we have a man who is a thinker and yet no sophist, no dreamer, but one who brings the full power of an inspired intelligence to bear upon the most urgent and the most momentous issues of life. In the evolution of this typical vital thinker as he comes before us in the words,

The Evolution of a Thinker

> "I thought on my ways,
> And turned my feet unto thy testimonies."

there are four things to be noted.

1. In the first place, his words are remarkable for the clear recognition which they contain of the supreme and ultimate relation of every human life. The last reference of our existence is to God. The words "my ways" and "thy testimonies" present the two terms in the great final comparison, the two persons, the finite and the infinite, who have to do with each other before all and after all. As a cathedral built in the heart of a great city rises with the other buildings round about it, keeps company with them a certain distance, and then leaves them all behind, soars away skyward, and at last, solitary and alone, looks up into the infinite spaces, so every man lives among men. He rests with them upon the same political and social foundation; he stands with them in a wide and important fellowship; he rises with them a certain way, and then he goes beyond them all, and the last look and reference of his spirit is to the

The Supreme Relation

Eternal. We drew our being from God, we live and move and have our being in God, and at death we breathe back our life into God's hands. The first thing in our existence is our Maker, and when we have done with all others we have still to do with him. For the clear and impressive recognition of this supreme and final relation of human life the words of the text are indeed remarkable. In the evolution of thought this thinker began at the divine beginning, and let us be thankful to him for that.

2. The words of this man are remarkable, in the second place, for the application which they reveal of an awakened intelligence to the business of living. Is it not strange that in a world where so much thinking is done, and where so many magnificent monuments have been erected to the triumph of human reason, so very little thought should be given to that which is of supreme moment—life itself? Every locomotive that leaves the station must have an engineer; that is, intelligence must be in command. Every ship that clears port

The Evolution of a Thinker

must have a captain; again, reason must rule. In all the professions the cry is for more light, for larger-minded men. And no one expects success anywhere in the business of the world but in proportion as he puts his mind upon his task. Our science, our art, our philosophy, our political institutions, our industry, our history, and our entire civilization are monuments of the greatness and triumph of the human mind. Upon every hand we behold the marvels achieved by thought. Everywhere it is doing wonders, except in the evolution of character. Life is left to make way for itself, to go unshielded into the field of battle. Character, the supreme thing, is abandoned to chance; it is left to grow wild; it is given no succor, no inspiration from the power of intelligence. And one may as reasonably expect a child to play in safety upon the confines of a jungle, with the hiss of the snake and the growl of the wild beast audible from the thicket, as for a young man to hope to keep his honor, maintain his purity, and hold fast his integrity in the peril of the world

A Typical Criticism

without the application of Christian intelligence to the business of living.

And this criticism holds against men of genius as well as against ordinary men. Like others, they are good and bad from impulse, and moral judgment has had but little to do with the guidance of their lives. Take, for example, the criticism that Burns passes upon himself in his poem "A Bard's Epitaph." How much deeper, how much more severe, how much more to the point it is than the censure of any other critic!

> "Is there a man whose judgment clear
> Can others teach the course to steer,
> Yet runs himself life's mad career
>   Wild as the wave?
> Here pause—and, through the starting tear,
>   Survey this grave."

> "The poor inhabitant below
> Was quick to learn and wise to know,
> And keenly felt the friendly glow
>   And softer flame;
> But thoughtless follies laid him low
>   And stain'd his name."

With what unerring insight the poet reaches to the heart of the difficulty, and with what

The Evolution of a Thinker

utter fidelity he lays it bare! The fundamental sin in the career of Burns was the failure to put his personal life under the power of moral intelligence. That, I do believe, is at the heart of the overwhelming majority of the blasted hopes and the blighted careers with which every fresh generation of young men has hitherto disappointed the world and plunged it in tears.

And even where thought is given to life, it is usually one-sided. There are two great partners in the business of living: the sum of things and the individual man; the universe and the single person; God and the soul. Two questions thus arise in every earnest mind: How does God deal with us? How do we behave toward God? Upon the first question we are marvelously free, and this may be one of the reasons for the amazing popularity in our time of the Book of Job. The absolute freedom of speech in which he indulges, the bold way in which he calls the Almighty to account, accords wonderfully well with our prevailing mood. We complain of the weather, which is not our work, but the Almighty's; we are vexed at our physical constitution, which is not of our doing, but of the divine; we are sore at heart—whatever we may pretend to the world—because we are so poorly endowed in intellect, which cannot be laid to our account, but must be laid at the door of our Maker; we are ashamed over the evil dispositions with which our nature is infested, and for which we are in no way responsible. We call God to account for our total inheritance and environment; we ask for light upon the mystery of iniquity and the mystery of pain.

All this freedom of thought is well. Let it go on. There is a fundamental faith in the reality of righteousness underneath it that makes it little short of a revelation of God. Theodicies have their necessity in the moral reason of man and in the conditions of the world. Sometimes they are a mere parade of rhetoric, like Pope's "Essay on Man"; again, they reduce themselves to nothing by denying the facts, like the optimism of Leib-

The Evolution of a Thinker

nitz; still further, they are epoch-making in their freedom, magnificence, and failure, like Job; and yet once more, they create new hope, as when Milton, on his way toward a justification of the ways of God to men, empties heaven and earth and hell in the presence of faith. Theodicies there have always been; attempts at them there always must be in this world. But the moment we throw the burden of human life, the world, the universe upon God we conquer ground for a new expectation. God will at last construct his own justification. And what a day that will be when the Eternal appears at the bar of the conscience that he has made and enlightened to give an account of his purpose in the universe! That will be the great and terrible day of the Lord. That is the final judgment toward which the conscience of man looks forward both with awe and with deathless desire. With such a cause, for such an end, with such a Reasoner, how ineffably solemn and grand the scene will be! Then surely the morning stars will renew and perfect their song, and

Man's Problem

all the sons of God will shout for joy as they never yet have done.

But if the universe has its problem, we have ours. It is our privilege to ask God to account to the conscience that he creates and trains for his conduct of the world. But here our solicitude should cease. We may rest assured that the Infinite will give his answer, that God will accomplish what it is his to accomplish. Meanwhile we have our fundamental question, How are we behaving toward the Eternal? Granted that the mystery of temptation, and hard tasks, and disagreeable circumstances, and positive disappointments, and occasional sweeping losses is for God to explain, is it not ours to play the man in all, under all, and through all? There are two questions that may be asked about the great Face in the Franconia Notch, the "Old Man of the Mountain." You may ask, How does the sky deal with the Face? Does it bite it with frost, does it snow it under, does it sweep it with storms, does it tread the great features with the feet of hurricanes,

The Evolution of a Thinker

does it greet it out of an endless succession of sunrises, does the glow of innumerable sunsets, reflected from the transfigured clouds that float before it, light up the lofty profile? That is one question. But there is another. How does the Face behave toward the sky? Is it calm and grand and fixed and serene, sublimely expectant, and in immortal reconciliation with the infinite, and in blessed peace? How is God dealing with you? What kind of blood has he poured into your veins? Of what tissue and substance has he made you, and what are the forms of trial with which he has girt you? What is your inheritance and what your environment? How is God dealing with you? That is one side of the business of living. But there is another. What is your bearing toward him? Are you a coward or a king, a devotee of indulgence or a hero of righteousness, a mutineer in the world or an unchangeable witness of love and hope?

3. This Hebrew thinker was remarkable for the way in which he discovered that he

The Power of the Bible

was wrong. He began to think upon his personal life, and he soon found that he was not the first nor the greatest thinker in that region. A royal succession had preceded him. They had recorded their thoughts upon the greatest interests of existence. Their recorded thoughts had become the highest wisdom, the Holy Scriptures, the Bible of the nation to which this man belonged. To these testimonies of God he turned, and these sustained, enlarged, and enlightened his best reflections upon his own life. He took his career to the highest, and in its presence he discovered the error in which he had been trying to live.

When a young man who is gifted as a musician goes to perfect his education, the nobler his nature and the more promising his mood, the more eager he is to live in the company of such musicians as Schubert, Mendelssohn, and Beethoven. These great kings in the realm of harmony are ever about him, ever looking down upon him, and his life is rebuked and corrected by them and inspired

The Evolution of a Thinker

at the same time. When a student of painting really wishes to excel, to discover his defect, and to see the path to high achievement, he goes to the great European galleries where the masters will look down upon him from the walls. In the presence of Rembrandt, Titian, and Raphael he will find both the error of his work and the way out of it. There these masters stand, forever revising, forever correcting, forever pointing out the defect and forever indicating the path to true achievement. Our own Longfellow, the most completely poetical nature that we have yet produced, owed his humility and his perfection as an artist in no small measure to the fact that he lived with Dante. The great Florentine revised and guided, rebuked and inspired his devoted scholar. And it is beautiful to think of Tennyson, the consummate poet and artist of our century, dying with Shakespeare in his hand, thus acknowledging his deep indebtedness to the high excellence of that supreme poetic genius.

Now when a man of the world wants to

Appeal to the Highest

test his goodness, what does he usually do? He picks out some shabby church-member and compares him with himself. Finding himself as good as the other member of the comparison,—he could not well be worse,— he congratulates himself and concludes that he is good enough. And so men who want excuses for their low lives take good men at their worst—Peter when he denied his Master, the ten when they forsook the Lord, Paul when he lost his temper—and again suborn their moral judgment. Take good men at their best; take the divine man Christ, and the error will soon leap to light. There is one hymn which we especially need to sing these days:

> "O God, how infinite art thou!
> What worthless worms are we!"

We need the sense of contrast between our wretched lives and God's perfections, between our poor, miserable actual and the blazing and eternal ideal. The highest wisdom of the race, the Bible, the highest life in history, the life of Christ,—hither we must come for the evolution of a true moral judgment upon our personal life.

4. Last of all, this man is remarkable for the ease with which, finding he was wrong, he returned to righteousness. He consulted the testimonies of God and found that he was wrong. Instantly the active power of his nature came into play: he turned his feet unto these same testimonies; he grasped the right thought of life; that right thought must be embodied in his heart, in his speech, in his whole existence. Show an honest man that he is wrong; if he sees it, and if he is an honest man, he will turn at once. If he is full of excuses he is a hypocrite. Take the difference between Paul and Felix. Paul, going like a cyclone against Christianity, against the great cause of humanity in his age, is met by the light from heaven. It struck him to the ground. He was spoken to by the Lord, and what is his cry? "What wilt thou have me to do?" The answer is, "Become an apostle; retrace your steps;

The Test of Sincerity

wherever you have persecuted my cause go and preach it." Instantly he rose up and went, and met the sneer and the scoff and the persecution of those who had hailed his fanaticism with joy, who now hated him because of his adoption of the new faith. By his immediate renunciation of a discovered error he showed his sincerity. He could not stand by a lie; he could not consecrate his power to that which God had demonstrated to his soul to be wrong. Take now the case of Felix. Paul preached to Felix on temperance and righteousness and judgment to come, and he trembled in his inmost soul at the power of that preaching. What was his response? "Go thy way for this time; when I have a convenient season, I will call for thee." He was a sneak! No other word describes it. Tell a man he is wrong; if he is a man, he will right it, by the help of God. Show a man that he is wrong, and if he begins to reason about it, give excuses for it, procrastinate and promise amendment by and by, that man is morally unsound to the cen-

The Evolution of a Thinker

ter of his soul. When the captain of a ship has been out at sea in a fog for a week, and has been going God only knows where, and suddenly the cloud lifts and the sun streams upon him, and he finds out that he is hundreds and hundreds of miles away from his true course, what does he do? He thanks God for deliverance, for the great rebuke, for the sweet discovery of the light, heads the ship the other way, and begins to beat back with a singing heart to his true course. And so when you find an honest man, and show him that he is not on the right path, that he has departed from his true course, gratitude leaps like a spring set free in his heart, and there is a new song in his soul, and he begins to beat back to righteousness.

These, then, are the four things to be laid to heart. First of all, we must recognize and revere our Maker. In the evolution of the thinker, we must begin at the beginning. We come from God, we go to God, and our entire existence is supported by his will. We must see him face to face; we must feel

The Great Opportunity

him under and over and round about and within our life. Our being must be ever open toward him, as the windows of the devout Jew in exile were toward Jerusalem. Our nature must become alive with his presence, our character all shot through with his power. Then we shall have a divinely illuminated intelligence to bring to bear upon the great business of living. Christian manhood will issue from the creative presence of the Eternal Spirit within the soul, mediated, understood, interpreted, and served by the whole power of reason. And in the companionship of the Lord the secret sin, the hidden fault, the entire defect and error of existence, will lie in perpetual open revelation. Last of all, we shall leap to the grandest privilege given to man, the sublime chance for the return to righteousness. I cannot tell you how very great human life seems to me to be under this conception. I have looked at the tide going seaward, at the ocean returning upon itself, until it seemed as if it would go away forever and come again no more. But the

The Evolution of a Thinker

moment of pause, change, and return finally arrived. First in ripples, then in heavier swells and longer rolls, with the constant retrograde constantly checked and overcome, with the pull of the heavens and the cry of the shore, it thundered to the flood at last. So we retreat from wisdom, from goodness, from God; and so we return when we come to ourselves. To beat back out of the depths and from the far distances, to come homeward in spite of all reverse movements, to rise to the flood at length—that is but a poor symbol for the march upon righteousness, the joy of the successive gains, and the hope of the final and overwhelming triumph in God.

The Great Heresy

By
David James Burrell, D.D.
Pastor of Marble Collegiate Church, New York City

"From that time forth began Jesus to show unto his disciples, how that he must go unto Jerusalem, and suffer many things of the elders and chief priests and scribes, and be killed, and be raised again the third day. Then Peter took him, and began to rebuke him, saying, Be it far from thee, Lord: this shall not be unto thee. But he turned, and said unto Peter, Get thee behind me, Satan: thou art an offense unto me: for thou savorest not the things that be of God, but those that be of men."—Matt. xvi. 21–23.

IN the religion of the Parsees there are two supreme beings: Ormuzd, "the Good," creator and sustainer of all things bright and helpful; and Ahriman, "the Black," who presides over the regions of darkness, evokes the malignant passions, and stands sponsor for war and sorrow, disease and death. These two are perpetually arrayed against each other, the

The Great Heresy

gage of conflict being the dominion of this world. It is like a stupendous game of chess, in which wars and truces, the convulsions of nature, and the ups and downs of history, are as the moves of pawns and castles upon the board. It is impossible to say how long the game will continue, or what the issue will be, inasmuch as the contestants are coeval and coequal. Perhaps it will go on forever.

We also believe in two great powers who contend for the sovereignty of this world, but they are not coequal. One is infinite; the other—though of immense guile and resource—is finite. And the end is to be seen from the beginning. God is always and everywhere getting the upper hand of Satan. The world grows constantly and cumulatively better from century to century, from year to year, from day to day. Every time our old world rolls around, it rolls a little farther into the light.

> "The eternal step of progress beats
> To that great anthem, calm and slow,
> Which God repeats.
> God works in all things; all obey

"Here am I; Send Me!"

> His first propulsion from the night.
> Wake thou and watch! The world is gray
> With morning light!"

There never was a moment, from the beginning of the eternal ages, when God did not intend to save this world. All things were included in his foreknowledge. Sin, suffering, salvation, the casting down of iniquity, and the restitution of all things in the fullness of time, were from eternity present before him. In one of the boldest and most picturesque portions of Scripture we are introduced into the councils of the ineffable Trinity. The three Persons are represented as in earnest conference respecting the deliverance of our sin-stricken race. The cry of the erring and suffering has come up into their ears. The inquiry is heard, "Whom shall we send, and who will go for us?" Then the only-begotten Son offers himself: "Here am I; send me!" He girds himself with omnipotence, binds upon his feet the sandals of salvation, and goes forth as a knight-errant to vindicate and rescue the children of men. When next we behold him he is a child, wrapped in swaddling-clothes and lying in a manger. The incarnation is the first chapter in his great undertaking, and a necessary part of it. As Anselm says in *Cur Deus Homo*—" He must become man in order to suffer, and he must continue to be God in order that he may suffer enough for all." In thus assuming our nature he laid aside the form of his Godhood and " the glory which he had with the Father before the world was "; but he never lost sight of his beneficent purpose. He realized constantly that he had come to redeem the world by dying for it.

In one of the earliest pictures of the nativity he is represented as lying in the manger, while just above him, on the wall of the stable, is the shadow of a cross. So Holman Hunt paints him in the carpenter shop: the day's work is over; the weary toiler lifts his arms in an attitude of utter weariness, and the level rays of the setting sun cast upon the wall yonder again the shadow of a cross.

"For This Cause Came I"

The suggestion is true: he was born under that shadow and lived under it. He knew that he had come to die. He knew that, inasmuch as the penalty had been passed upon the race, "The soul that sinneth, it shall die," there could be no deliverance but by death. *Mors janua vitæ.*

A company of Greeks, on one occasion, came, saying, "We would see Jesus." He kept them waiting while he uttered those apparently inconsequential words, "Now is my soul troubled." Why should his soul be troubled? Because he saw in those waiting Greeks the vanguard of a great multitude who were to come to him as the fruit of the travail of his soul. At that moment he felt himself passing under the shadow of the cross —deeper, darker than ever—to pay ransom for these seeking ones. He shrank from the bitterness of his approaching death, yet knew it to be necessary for the success of his errand: "Now is my soul troubled; and what shall I say? *Father, save me from this hour?* Nay, but for this cause came I unto this hour.

The Great Heresy

Father, glorify thy name!" He had come to die for sinners. It must needs be. He knew that without his vicarious death the guilty race was without hope. He must give "his soul an offering for sin."

It could not be supposed, however, that Satan, the prince of this world, would suffer his power to slip away without a desperate effort to retain it. He would put forth every energy and use every means to thwart the beneficent purpose of Christ. Thus we account for those extraordinary manifestations of malignant energy, during the years of Christ's ministry, known as "demoniacal possession." Wherever a soul was open and willing to be used there the adversary entered in. The plans of Jesus must be overturned; he must not be permitted to ransom the world; he must not die for it.

Out in the wilderness, after the forty days of fasting, the adversary met Jesus and presented to his weak and suffering soul the great temptation. He led him to a high place and, with a wave of the hand, directed

"Get Thee Behind Me, Satan!"

his thought to all the kingdoms of this world, saying, "All these are mine. I know thy purpose: thou art come to win this world by dying for it. Why pay so great a price? I know thy fear and trembling—for thou art flesh—in view of the nails, the fever, the dreadful exposure, the long agony. *Why pay so great a price?* I am the prince of this world. One act of homage and I will abdicate! Fall down and worship me!" Never before or since has there been such a temptation, so specious, so alluring. But Jesus had covenanted to die for sinners. He knew there was really no other way of accomplishing salvation for them. He could not be turned aside from the work which he had volunteered to do. Wherefore he put away the alluring suggestion with the word, "Get thee behind me, Satan! I cannot be moved. I know the necessity that is laid upon me. I know that my way to the kingdom is only by the cross. I am therefore resolved to suffer and die for the deliverance of men."

The stress of this temptation was over; but

The Great Heresy

once and again it returned, as when, after a memorable day of preaching and wonder-working, his followers proposed to lead him to Jerusalem and place him upon the throne of David (John vi. 15); and he "departed into a mountain alone."

We now come to the immediate occasion of our context. Jesus, with his disciples, was on his last journey to Jerusalem—that memorable journey of which it is written, "He set his face steadfastly" toward the cross. He had been with his disciples now three years, but had not been able to fully reveal his mission, because they were not strong enough to bear it. A man with friends, yet friendless, lonely in the possession of his great secret, he had longed to give them his full confidence, but dared not venture. Now, as they journeyed southward through Cæsarea Philippi, he asked them, "Who do men say that I am?" And they answered, "Some say John the Baptist; some, Elias: others, Jeremias, or one of the prophets." And he saith, "But who say ye that I am?" Then Peter

"Get Thee Behind Me, Satan!"

—brave, impulsive, glorious Peter—witnessed his good confession: "Thou art the Christ, the Son of the living God." The hour had come! His disciples were beginning to know him. He would give them his full confidence. So as they journeyed toward Jerusalem he told them all—how he had come to redeem the world by bearing its penalty of death; "he began to show them, how he must suffer many things of the elders and chief priests and scribes, and be killed." At that point Peter could hold his peace no longer, but began to rebuke him, saying, "Be it far from thee, Lord! To suffer? To die? Nay, to reign in Messianic splendor!" And Jesus, turning, said unto Peter, "Get thee behind me, Satan!"—the very words with which he had repelled the same suggestion in the wilderness. As he looked on his disciple he saw not Peter, but Satan—perceived how the adversary had for the moment taken possession, as it were, of this man's brain and conscience and lips. "Get thee behind me, Satan! I know thee; I recognize thy crafty suggestion; but I am not to be turned aside from my purpose. Get thee behind me! Thou art an offense unto me. Thy words are not of divine wisdom, but of human policy. Thou savorest not the things that be of God, but those that be of men!"

We are now ready for our proposition, which is this: *The vicarious death of Jesus is the vital center of the whole Christian system; and any word which contravenes it is in the nature of a satanic suggestion.* There is one truth before which all other truths whatsoever dwindle into relative insignificance, to wit, that our Lord Jesus Christ was wounded for our transgressions and bruised for our iniquities, that by his stripes we might be healed. The man who apprehends this by faith is saved by it.

And contrariwise, any denial of this truth is mortal heresy. The first satanic suggestion made to man was a denial of the law, when the tempter said to Adam, " Thou shalt not surely die." The last satanic suggestion is a denial of grace: " It is not necessary that

A Satanic Suggestion

Christ should die for thee." The first ruined the race, and the last will destroy any man who entertains it.

The suggestion comes in various ways, as when it is said that the gospel is not the only religion that saves: "If a man is sincere, what difference does it make?

> 'For forms of faith let canting bigots fight,
> His faith cannot be wrong whose life is right.'

Here is a Confucianist bowing before his ancestral tablets; here is a Brahman bathing in his sacred river; and here an African bowing before his fetish. All these are sincere; shall they not be saved with us?" If so, then the death of the Lord Jesus Christ, the only-begotten Son of the Father, was an incomprehensible waste of divine resource, and there is no significance in the word that is written: "There is none other name under heaven given among men, whereby we must be saved."

It is said again, that we are saved by the life of the Lord Jesus Christ as an example of holiness, leading us on to self-culture and

The Great Heresy

character-building, and his death has practically nothing to do with our entrance into life. If that is true, then Christ did but mock our infirmity in setting up such an ideal. He did indeed come into the world to tell us how men ought to live, what a true man ought to be, what character means. That was incidental to his great redemptive mission, leading us on from deliverance to righteousness. But if that were all, then I say he mocked our infirmity. For there is not an earnest man who does not kneel down beside his bed at night, after his most strenuous effort to imitate Christ, and say, "Have mercy upon me, O Lord, for I have sinned." We have all sinned and come short of the glory of God.

Again, it is said that Christ did not die vicariously, under the burden of sin, taking our place before the offended law, but died as all martyrs die. "He came into the world as a reformer, to overthrow the evil condition of things, and suffered the fate of all earnest souls. He gathered into his de-

The Voice of Scripture

voted heart the shafts of the adversary, and fell." If that be so, what is the meaning of the constant statement that the death of Jesus Christ was a voluntary death? The Father gave him, he gave himself, an offering for sin. "I have power to lay down my life, and I have power to take it again; no man taketh my life from me." Life was his; he made it; he played with it as little children play with their toys.

1. To deny this doctrine of the vicarious atonement, in any of these ways or otherwise, is to set one's self athwart the whole trend of Scripture. For from Genesis to Revelation there is a thoroughfare stained with the blood that cleanseth from sin. No sooner had man sinned than the protevangel spoke of the "Seed of the woman" suffering for it. The first altar, reared by the closed gate of paradise, prophesied of the slain Lamb of God. As the years passed the prophets declared, with ever-increasing clearness and particularity, the coming sacrifice. David sang of it in his Messianic psalms. Isaiah drew

The Great Heresy

the portrait of the agonizing Christ as if he had gazed on the cross: "He is . . . a man of sorrows, and acquainted with grief. . . . Surely he hath borne our griefs, and carried our sorrows. . . . And the Lord hath laid on him the iniquity of us all." The same truth was emphasized by Moses, Daniel, Zechariah, all the prophets down to Malachi, who, waving his torch in the twilight of the long darkness which closed the old economy, said, "The Sun of righteousness shall arise with healing in his wings." Open the Book where you will, the face of Jesus, so marred more than any man's, yet divinely beautiful, looks out upon you.

The rites and symbols of the Old Testament all find their fulfilment in Christ crucified. Their center was the tabernacle. Enter it and observe how it is everywhere sprinkled with blood. Here is blood flowing down the brazen altar, blood on the ewer, the golden candlestick, the table of showbread, the altar of incense; blood on the floor, the ceiling, on posts and pillars, on knops and blossoms, everywhere. Lift the curtain and pass into the holiest of all—but not without blood on your palms. Here is blood on the ark of the covenant, blood on the mercy-seat—blood, blood everywhere. What does it mean? Nothing, absolutely nothing, unless it declares the necessity of the cross. It is an empty dumb-show except as it points the worshiper to Him whose vicarious death is the only means of our salvation.

Wherefore I say the man who denies this truth must set himself against the sum and substance of the Scriptures. For if the atoning death of Christ be taken out of that blessed Book it is of no more value than a last year's almanac as a solution of the great problem of life.

2. Again, a denial of this doctrine involves a downright rejection of the philosophy of history.

The world has been growing better ever since the cross first cast its luminous shadow over it. Progress is a fact—a fact that must be accounted for. Hume undertook to write

The Great Heresy

history without Christ, and found it a labyrinth without a clue. So did Gibbon. They saw civilization advancing through the centuries, but, rejecting Christ, they could perceive no reason for it. The "logic of events" was nothing to them. There can, indeed, be no "philosophy of history" for a man who refuses to see Constantine's cross in the heavens, with its great prophecy, "*In hoc signo.*" It is a miraculous coincidence that the limits of civilization on earth to-day are coextensive with the charmed circle known as *Christendom.* "The world before Christ," says Luthardt, "was a world without love." The church with the proclamation of Christ, and him crucified, has come down through the centuries, like Milton's angel, with the torch; and all along the way have sprung up institutions of learning and charity and righteousness. The cross is the vital power of civilization. "All the light of sacred" and of secular story as well "gathers round its head sublime." If the world grows better, it is because Christ died for it.

The Consensus

3. Still further, to deny the vital importance of the vicarious death of Jesus is to contradict the universal instinct.

The doctrine of the redemptive power of substitutionary pain is not our exclusive property. It has, indeed, a place in all, or nearly all, the false religions. It may be dimly seen in the hammer of Thor; in the wounded foot of Brahma treading on the serpent; in the fable of Prometheus, bound to the Caucasus with a vulture at his vitals, and lamenting, " I must endure this until one of the gods shall bear it for me." It is still more evident in the institution of the sacrifice. Wherever a living thing is slain upon the altar, it means vicarious expiation, or else it means nothing at all.

And why should it be thought strange that God should send his only-begotten Son to suffer in our stead? Is not sympathy the noblest as well as the commonest thing in human experience? Men are suffering everywhere and always for other men. Parents are suffering for their children. The pains which we all endure are, for the most part, not the consequence of our own acts. At this point of sympathy our nature reaches its noblest and best. We esteem above all the unselfish man who voluntarily bears the burdens of others. Should we not, then, expect something of the same sort in our Father? He made us in his likeness. It would be monstrous if God did not sympathize with his children who have fallen into trouble. The cross is the very highest expression of sympathy in the universe. The atonement is what we should expect. It is just like God.

And it is God's exact response to the universal need. It fits our circumstances. As Coleridge said, "The gospel finds me." It answers the deepest longing of earnest souls. Dr. Chamberlain relates that among those converted by his preaching at the sacred city of Benares was a devotee who had dragged himself many miles upon his knees and elbows to bathe in the Ganges. He had at the bottom of his heart the common conviction of

Spes Unica

sin and desire of cleansing. "If I can but reach the Ganges," he thought, "this shame and bondage and fear will be taken away." Weak and emaciated from his long pilgrimage, he dragged himself down to the river's edge and, praying to Gunga, crept into it; then withdrawing, he lay upon the river's bank and moaned, "The pain is still here!" At that moment he heard a voice from the shadow of a banyan-tree near by. It was the missionary telling the story of the cross. The devotee listened, drank it in, rose to his knees, then to his feet; then, unable to restrain himself, he clapped his hands and cried, "That's what I want! That's what I want!" It is what we all want; the whole creation has from time immemorial groaned and travailed for it.

And it is our only hope. There are other religions and other philosophies, but none that suggests a rational plan of pardon for sin. *Spes unica.* I remember an old crucifix, in the public square of a Brittany village, which no one passed without bending the knee.

The Great Heresy

Workmen on their way to the fields, little children going to school, all bowed before that stone figure of the Christ, which the storms of centuries had worn almost out of human semblance. The last night, as I was leaving the village in the twilight, I saw an old woman bent almost prostrate before it. Her hands were clasped; her uplifted face bore the marks of suffering. I could not know the bitterness of that poor heart, but her eyes were turned toward the infinite Source of help and consolation. The dear hand upon the cross lifts every burden, heals every wound, and saves us from the penalty, the shame, and the bondage of sin.

And this is why we preach Christ, and him crucified. "There is none other name under heaven given among men, whereby we must be saved." "He was wounded for our transgressions, he was bruised for our iniquities; . . . and with his stripes we are healed." He is thus made unto us wisdom and righteousness and sanctification and redemption. He is first, last, midst, and all in all.

Christ Seeking the Lost

By
George Harris, D.D.
Professor of Theology in Andover Theological Seminary

"For the Son of man came to seek and to save that which was lost."—Luke xix. 10.

THIS sentence, which is so familiar, and which puts into a single phrase the whole gospel, occurs only once in the New Testament, in the narrative which describes the interview of Jesus with Zacchæus, the publican with whom Jesus dined in Jericho. In the revised version of the New Testament the saying is omitted from the report of Christ's words about little children where it occurs in the received version, and we may be glad that it is omitted there. For children are not lost. When they are men and women they may be lost, but as children they are not lost. But Zacchæus was regarded by the

Christ Seeking the Lost

people of Jericho as lost. He was a despised man. There was no salvation for him. Yet Jesus, seeing the penitence and generosity of the man, exclaimed, "To-day is salvation come to this house." He may really have been lost before he knew Jesus, but Jesus came and saved him.

1. Who are the lost? What is it to be lost? We suppose the lost are those who fail of heaven, who finally are in the outer darkness. But that is merely the end. They will not be lost at last unless they were lost before. Jesus spoke of those who were lost then—people all about him, with whom he conversed on the streets and in their homes. Because they already were lost he came to save them; not merely to keep them from being lost by and by, but to recover them from the lost state in which they then were, to save that which *was* lost. If it was so then it doubtless is so now.

He took pains to explain by parables what it is to be lost, and we can understand best by taking his own illustrations:

Three Parables

A lost sheep, one from a flock of a hundred, gone astray in the wilderness;

A lost coin, one out of ten pieces of silver a woman had, which had rolled away into some crevice;

A lost son, one of two, who had become dissipated and was in a far country, poor and destitute.

These three illustrations, explaining what it is to be lost, constitute the whole of that pathetic, tender, hopeful fifteenth chapter of Luke's gospel.

A lost sheep is not destroyed, has not been killed and eaten by the wolf. Its value remains. The fleece may be torn by briers, but is still fine and heavy. It has gone astray, has wandered farther and farther away from home, and does not know the way back. In the forest, among the rocks, with no familiar object, no trodden path to be seen, the poor animal runs hither and thither, pitifully bleating, helpless, frightened, lost. Have you ever been lost in a forest? You have been following a path, but it becomes narrow

Christ Seeking the Lost

and indistinct till at last it disappears altogether. You do not know what direction you should take. You wander aimlessly about. At length you find footprints and follow them, only to see after a while that they are your own tracks. Daylight dies away. In the twilight the trees seem to be moving giants. Strange sounds startle you. The deeper shadows fall; the gloom is impenetrable. You are utterly bewildered, till at last, exhausted and alarmed, you lean against a tree or sink to the ground, knowing that you are lost.

Jesus was thinking of those who had wrong ideas of God, who were lost in a maze of ceremonials and observances which did not satisfy their need of God; and was thinking of those who had strayed from the path of rectitude and purity and did not know the way back to their true life as trusting, obedient children of God. They reminded him of sheep lost in the wilderness. "When he saw the multitudes, he was moved with compassion for them, because they were distressed

Doubt and Despair

and scattered, as sheep not having a shepherd."

If one is perplexed with doubts concerning God's love, or even his very existence, asking, as he sees the evils of the world and suffers the disappointments and pains of his own life, "Is there a God after all?" if one can find no meaning in life, if he doubts or dreads a life beyond, and wishes with a sigh that he had a simple, unquestioning faith in God, that one is lost—not lost beyond recovery, but lost in the wilderness, not knowing the way back, the way home. If one has not kept his virtue, if by self-indulgence he has made himself coarse, has forfeited his self-respect, and feels that he has no right to associate with good men and pure women, is full of bitter self-reproach, would give anything if he had not so sinned, but does not know how to recover himself, he is lost—not, as he may suppose, beyond hope, but he is wandering farther away from goodness, or in his own old tracks, and cannot find the way back.

Christ Seeking the Lost

A lost coin, a lost piece of silver, is in existence, represents value, but is covered with dust on the floor, or is in some dark corner, and so is useless. The owner has lost the use of it. That is precisely the way in which a great many people are lost. They are lost to their right uses. They either are doing nothing, sauntering through life blameless and good-natured enough, or are living on some low plane of selfishness to get gain and spend it on themselves. It is said, "What a pity that a young man of his talents, education, property, is a mere pleasure-seeker!" He has rolled into some narrow social crevice, or has degraded himself to company only with sporting men,—a piece of silver in a dust-heap,—and is wasting his life on trivial interests. God has lost him, the world has lost him, for they have no use of him. He is lost to his right uses. In the disuse or misuse of his powers he is lost in some dirty corner, in which there must be diligent sweeping to find him at all, to find that he still exists.

A Lost Son

And a lost son, one of two—a prodigal son. This is not so much an illustration as an instance. The prodigal was not *like* a lost man, he *was* a lost man. He was lost to his father. There was no companionship, no affection, no obedience. He might as well not have been. It was as if he had been dead, just as his father said when the son returned: "He was dead." And he was lost to himself, to his true self. Instead of being what he might have been in purity, honor, manliness, he was intemperate and licentious. The true self, the real man, had been usurped by the false self, the ruined man. So one may be lost to his heavenly Father, as he certainly is if by a selfish and dissolute life he is lost to his earthly father. God, who desires the trust, obedience, and affection of his child, receives no sign, no prayer, no service. God has lost his own child. One may be lost to himself even if he has not plunged into the gross sins of sensuality and lust. In the low life of pleasure and frivolity, without high aims and noble ambitions, the mean,

Christ Seeking the Lost

narrow, selfish man has banished the true, pure, magnanimous, gentle man. Why, here was a boy of sweet nature, open, bright face, quick intellect, upon whom great hopes were placed. It was expected that he would become a good man, a useful man, a respected and honored man, a religious man. But that boy has become a hard, contemptuous, vain, coarse, and vicious man, and the man that might have been is lost. He is not his true and proper self. No wonder, when the prodigal thought of what he might have been and of what he was, and determined to go home, it is said that he came to himself. It seems a contradiction when it is remarked of one that he is not himself; yet how often the vices, follies, infatuations of men oblige us to say just that!

So one is lost when he is wandering in error, doubt, perplexity, like a lost sheep; lost when he is not put to his right uses, like a lost coin; lost when friendship and affection have nothing from him, when God has nothing from him, when he is lost to himself, like

Christ Saving the Lost

a spendthrift who has wasted his substance in riotous living, a lost son. If this is what it is to be lost, then, alas! some are lost now, long before the day of judgment.

2. The Son of man came to *save* that which was lost. He would recover a man to himself, to his uses, and so to God. He knew that in men, even those considered very wicked, there was power of recuperation, power of recovery. So he came to bring to them that truth, that influence, that life, that love, on which they still could fasten, and which could restore them to themselves, to their uses, and to God. If only they would believe him and would trust him and would try, they could be saved.

There are many saviors in the world. A good friend who will not give a man up when he has gone astray, who throws the protection of a generous friendship around him, saves one who otherwise might be lost. A father, a mother, has saved a child by letting the child see what a true life is, by making a child know that even if he should go astray he

Christ Seeking the Lost

would be welcomed back. The prodigal knew his father well enough to know that, and that was what brought him home. The world is full of saving forces as well as of destroying forces. It has been said, "You may save any one if you will love him enough." The saviors are those who have the spirit of Christ, who, knowing it or not knowing it, feel somewhat as he did toward men, never despairing of them, ready to suffer for them and with them.

How did Christ save men? How did he save Zacchæus, for instance? He saved Zacchæus simply by telling him that he would take dinner with him and by actually going to his house to dine. Not a reputable man in Jericho would have done that, would have put himself on a social equality with that despised and hated man who had become rich by extorting heavy taxes from the people. When this undersized man—a dwarf, perhaps—saw Jesus, whose very presence and bearing showed him noble and compassionate, yet unswerving in righteousness and com-

Received Him Joyfully

manding in moral authority, and when he heard his own name with the request for hospitality, the man's heart leaped for joy; there was hope for him. "And he made haste, and came down, and received him joyfully." How much that act of gracious courtesy meant and cost to Jesus is not overlooked in the story. "And when they saw it, they all murmured,"—all of them,—"saying, He is gone in to lodge with a man that is a sinner." Little cared Zacchæus for that. For once in his life he was well treated by one whose regard he cared for. He was saved,—saved to himself and to his uses,—and he at once consecrated his wealth to the good of men.

Jesus saved men by making them understand about God. "God feels toward you," he said, "as I feel. He loves you, cannot bear to lose you." Some way they did understand when they knew Jesus, as the world has been understanding ever since, and the doubts, the errors, the perplexities vanish, the sins are forsaken, the life of useful service is begun; we know ourselves children of

God; we are carried home on Christ's strong shoulders.

3. But this is not all. The Son of man came to *seek* that which was lost. He did not wait for men to make their painful way to him, and so to perish if they should not find him, to say nothing of those who do not know they are lost and do not even try to find a Saviour. He came to *seek* that which was lost, to make *his* mighty way to them through all obstacles and all indifference. He was engaged in a holy, loving search for lost souls, with an eagerness which could not fail to find them.

When he taught and preached he was seeking men. He scanned every company of hearers, searching for the responsive faces, the wistful, earnest faces, and addressed himself to them, as every real teacher and preacher looks among the upturned faces before him for those who respond to his words. Then he would seek out privately one and another whom he had noticed listening eagerly. In the throng around him

The Loving Search

at Jericho he saw one of the kind he sought looking down on him out of the branches of a shade-tree by the wayside.

But words and precepts even from the great Teacher may fall unheeded—heard, indeed, but not understood. He sought men by healings, by the cure of bodily ills, to get at their souls afterward, as in the case of the blind man whom he afterward found in the temple; he had been looking for him and at last found him.

He sought them in their homes, dined with them, conversed with them one by one, taking great risks to himself, if need be, so that he might get at them.

He sought them by his living, by showing them the true life of purity, of courage, of sympathy, so different from the hard, contemptuous, selfish life of their religious teachers.

He sought them by dying; he gave up his life because he would not be turned away from that holy search for the lost and despised. Even on the cross the search did not cease, for there he found and saved the penitent thief.

Ever since, and now, Christ is seeking men,

is seeking us, making his way to us through our prejudices, doubts, unbelief, and sin till he stands before us. Sometimes one has a thought of his true self, of what he might have been, ought to have been. "Oh, if I could only live my life over again!" he says, and says it while he is still young in years. Thinking thus, he is ashamed of himself as he is, yet does not know how to recover, or believes he cannot recover, that true self. You are the very man Christ is seeking. In that thought, that longing, that regret he has found you, and he is saying to you, "Wouldst thou be made whole?" If you will trust yourself to him, venturing out on him, you will regain what you have lost and will be a man in Christ Jesus.

You have been living all to yourself, planning your life so as to get pleasure and gain for your own enjoyment. You are conscious of powers by which you can succeed in your selfish ambitions. You think you can hold your own in the fierce competition. But sometimes you see that your powers can be

Saved to One's Uses

used in a better way. You see a world of need, suffering, ignorance, which are largely due to selfish strife. You hear the call to service. You see that the truly great men, the really good men, have devoted their gifts, attainments, knowledge to the service of others, and that such men as you are proposing to yourself to be have only made the world worse. Who of you has not had such thoughts of a noble, useful life? Again, you are the man Christ is seeking. In those thoughts he has found you. He would have you act on those convictions, would save you thus to your right uses, to which you now are lost in wrong and selfish uses.

Or, it does not seem real to you that there is a God, or, if there is, that he knows you or has anything to do with you. You seem insignificant in this vast universe, lost in the very greatness of the world, swept along, a helpless atom, by its resistless, unfeeling forces. You are like one lost in a dark, vast forest, with no sun, no star even, to guide you. And you are far away from God by

Christ Seeking the Lost

your sins. You say you cannot pray now as you could when you were a child. At the beginning of a day you cannot ask God's blessing on what you know you will do; at the end of a day you would be ashamed to bring it to God. You see no path of life which does not end in darkness or in danger. Again, you are the man Christ is seeking. Thank God that you think sometimes of him, that you are not stolid, that you are not satisfied to be lost in his world and a wanderer from his ways. Jesus says, " God is not far away, a great power regardless of you. He is very near you. God is love. If you know me, you know God, the heart of God. I came right out from God to find you. See my life, my love, my compassion, my hope for you, and you see God, who is my Father and your Father. You know what God would have your life be. He would have it like mine. Come into that life and you are back in your Father's house. Come to yourself and you come to God. Come unto me and you shall find rest unto your soul."

Seeking All and Seeking Each

We think that by and by, when we become religious, God will be with us. But he is with us now, in every desire for goodness, in every regret for wrong, in the wish to be of service in the world, in the desire to recover the true self in character. If we did not have such desires and regrets we should be lost indeed. If we do not act on them we shall remain lost to ourselves, to our right uses, and to God.

The shepherd out in the wilderness to find one sheep out of a great flock of a hundred shows that God seeks each one of us, no matter how many there are nor how vast the world is; and so of one piece of silver out of ten. The love of the father for one son out of only two shows how much he cares for each of us. God does not forget you, but seeks you in Christ to save you, if you are only one out of a hundred or more. God in Christ loves you and seeks you to save you as earnestly as if he had only two sons and you were one of those two.

An Extraordinary Saint

By

William R. Richards, D.D.
Pastor of the Crescent Avenue Presbyterian Church, Plainfield, N. J.

" And the Spirit of the Lord came mightily upon him, and he rent him as he would have rent a kid, and he had nothing in his hand: but he told not his father or his mother what he had done."—Judges xiv. 6.

SAMSON—the most extraordinary character in the whole catalogue of saints. We are puzzled to see how he deserves to be called a saint; yet there stands his name, canonized in the Epistle to the Hebrews: " Gideon, Barak, Samson "—one of the heroes of the faith.

It is a hundred years, perhaps, since Gideon, the great judge, broke the power of the Midianites. The tribes of Israel, united for a little by his valor, had soon fallen asunder after

Philistines

his death, once more an easy prey to any new enemy. The most formidable of the new enemies were the Philistines, a race of strangers from nobody knows where, who had established themselves in the lowlands to the southwest of Canaan. A dull, heavy, slow-witted people, but of great bodily strength and devoted to war, they had completely subdued the southern part of Canaan, reducing the wretched Hebrews there to such a state of dependence that now they could not even get a plow sharpened without going down to some smith among the Philistines.

It was a happy stroke of wit on the part of the German student who fastened this name "Philistine" to the townspeople round about the university—the uncultured but prosperous middle classes, whom the poor scholar or artist cringes to and laughs at by turns. Well, such was this race which had now humiliated poor Israel. For several generations to come the struggle for national existence will be against them, culminating

An Extraordinary Saint

at last in the glorious and triumphant career of David.

Now it was Samson who began the resistance which David brought to such grand conclusion, and so we can understand how for Hebrew patriots ever after the name of Samson shared the glory of his more illustrious successor. His story reads like a series of martial songs, and perhaps that is what much of it is—a series of martial songs rather than prose record; but whether you read it or sing it, the story is wonderfully interesting and may be profitable.

I say we can easily understand how the name of this fearless champion against the Philistines should become glorious in patriotic song and story. What possible religious significance it has is not so clear. Yet the tale is told religiously. This child had been supernaturally promised to his parents, we read, and no doubt in answer to prayer. The parents were to bring him up as a Nazarite. In those days of disorder the Hebrews do not seem to have followed the strict

A Nazarite

rules of their law concerning things clean and unclean,—if, indeed, those laws were yet enacted in their later form,—but this child must follow them; he must be as one separate from others in touching no unclean thing. Beyond that, he must drink no wine nor strong drink, and no razor must ever come upon his head. Those were the rules of the Nazarites.

So there was something religious in him—this quality of separateness. The length of his hair—a curious mark of physical prowess recently revived—was important as a chief token of this Nazarite separateness. Moreover, he must drink no wine nor strong drink. I do not suppose the Hebrew writer or reader connected that rule with the dangers of intoxication, but we cannot fail to do so to-day, knowing what we now know of alcohol and its effects on the human system. Is it not startling that this old Nazarite regulation has slowly got itself established as a rule of training for every modern Samson who wishes to excel in strength? As Milton puts it grandly in his poem:

An Extraordinary Saint

> "O madness, to think use of strongest wines
> And strongest drinks our chief support of health,
> When God with these forbidden made choice to rear
> His mighty champion, strong above compare,
> Whose drink was only from the liquid brook."

So Samson grew up a Nazarite from birth, and these Nazarite peculiarities made him a sort of religious personage; but, except for these peculiarities, he was as little like what we call religious as anything you could well conceive: a strong, fearless, irrepressible boy and lad and youth, true to his Nazarite vow, but in other things which we should deem more important setting no bridle to his lusts, and, above all, overflowing with a quality which we seldom associate with the Hebrew race; for the amazing strength of this man is not a more conspicuous trait in him than his rollicking humor. His story is the one part of the Bible which bubbles over with irrepressible fun. A big, overgrown boy, life was one long joke to him until it was darkened by his great disaster; and even then, the ruling passion strong in death, he contrived to make the last tragedy itself a kind of ap-

His Good Humor

palling jest, for he first got his enemies roaring with laughter before he pulled down the roof on their heads. Whether he was proposing riddles at his own wedding to his Philistine groomsmen; or, when he lost his wager, paying it to the winners with the spoil of some of their own friends whom he slew for the purpose; or turning into their fields of grain a lot of jackals with blazing torches tied to their tails, that he might look on from the hillside and see the manifold devastation spreading itself among the grain and laugh at the comical disaster; or choosing a jaw-bone of an ass to slay Philistines with, and celebrating the fight in a song, and naming the place from that extraordinary weapon—in all his encounters with these heavy-witted foes Samson contrived to attain two objects: he got his revenge on them and he got his laugh out of them. The physical strength and the cheerful good humor of the youth were alike unconquerable, and it is an interesting fact that the scholars are in some doubt whether his name means strong or sunny.

An Extraordinary Saint

Reading the Bible with our Puritan associations and antecedents, we have not always appreciated this feature of the story. Our Samson is rather the Samson Agonistes of Milton's poem, a splendid poetic creation, but by no means the same man with this Samson of the Book of Judges; for John Milton, Puritan that he was, had little time for laughter. His hero moves on sedately in majestic blank verse, fit captain for some regiment of solemn-visaged Ironsides; but the real Samson laughed himself out of his cradle, and through one chapter of his life into another, and into his grave at last.

We thank God for our Puritan ancestry and for their solemn, steadfast righteousness; but I thank God also that the inspired list of saints finds room, somewhere between Enoch and Moses and Samuel and all the prophets, for poor Samson, the sunny and the strong. So, then, this element of humor and fun is not all of the devil, though the evil one may have contrived to appropriate such large tracts of it for his uses. There is a great

Because Ye are Strong

deal of jesting that the apostle calls foolish and not convenient; those who make a mock at sin are fools; it is the laughter of fools that is like the crackling of thorns under a pot; the beatitude is for those who mourn. Yet in spite of all this, the Bible also sets forward this other side of the truth and tells how God himself can fill men's souls with joy and laughter, and that his appointed champion may be the sunny and strong.

"I write unto you, young men, because ye are strong," says the apostle; not in spite of your strength and all those cheerful elements of soul which compose it—not in spite of it, but because ye are strong and sunny-hearted. Behold this champion whose name would cheer the Hebrews through generations of hard struggle against the terrible Philistines to final victory over them, because God had given him such mighty strength and such healthy and resolute and infectious good humor. "I write unto you, young men, because ye are strong"; and remember these same qualities of youthful strength and

An Extraordinary Saint

good humor and natural, happy hopefulness ought to be serving some good purpose in the Lord's campaign against sin, putting heart into your sadder neighbors to fight on the same side.

But I would not leave the impression that this story of Samson is altogether pleasant reading. It ought to be, but much of it is not—quite the reverse; it is laughable, but it is very sad. His life-story is so nearly a failure. So far our English poet was justified in making it the basis of a tragedy. With all his strength he was so pitiably weak. Samson had his laugh out of the Philistine men, but their sisters avenged them on him, making a slave and tool and fool of him. The old writer tells his tale straight on without stopping to moralize much, but where can you find a sermon on the need of personal purity like this—so magnificently strong, so fatally and contemptibly weak? Of the two forms of sin which specially assail young men, Samson may guard us from the one by way of example, and from the other by

Purity

way of warning. Touching no wine, he excelled in strength; but he listened to Delilah, and there quickly followed weakness, darkness, the prison-house, the grave. A giant for muscle, but not a strong man all round. He was a weakling beside that hero of Tennyson's who could say:

> "My good blade carves the casques of men;
> My tough lance thrusteth sure;
> My strength is as the strength of ten,
> Because my heart is pure."

But it would be a great mistake to suppose that Samson's only fault was his susceptibility to woman's beauty. That became a fatal blemish in his character because of something else that was amiss in him, or lacking in him. His great fault was of omission more than of commission. The reason why he followed after that which was evil was that he lacked something else to follow after—something that was good. Beyond the mere obedience to his Nazarite vow, can you point out a single ennobling purpose in this man's life, a single persistent purpose of any sort, except

An Extraordinary Saint

to get his own amusement out of life as he went through it? He shows a kind of patriotism, perhaps, but of no very exalted quality; for it appears that this valiant Hebrew slew Philistines chiefly for purposes of his own, to satisfy his own grudges. No doubt God might use the man's exploits afterward for rousing Israel and encouraging her against her foes. But Samson himself betrays no such large purpose or expectation; he was avenging himself, that was all, or else amusing himself.

Ah, young men, rejoice in your strength, and laugh, if you will, when your hearts are glad; but it is a sad thing to pass through this world with nothing better to do than laughing; and the more strength, the worse for you, perhaps, if you can find no good purpose to serve with it. You see a young man developing physical prowess in his games, and so long as the game lasts you are satisfied if he fairly wins; but what a melancholy failure the life seems if that young Hercules carries out into the world that splendid phy-

Want of Purpose

sique, but finds nothing there to do with it, no sort of man's work to make this world happier and better, nothing but to go on amusing himself all his days, until he falls victim to some fatal dissipation! Or even if it be strength of mind that his studies have developed in him, how far is that better than strength of body if the man finds no manly work to do with it, no deliberate campaign for Israel against the Philistines, nothing but to go on amusing himself with his strength all his days? What Samson teaches us by way of warning is that we must get something which he had not—some steadfast, ennobling purpose worthy of whatever strength God has given us. That is the safeguard against temptation. Delilah would have had little chance at the hero if he had had something to do. Laughter is to cheer a man in his work, not to take the place of his work. Games and sports are for the spare holiday, or for evening's refreshment when day's task is done; the long day itself is not a game or a joke. "They that sow in tears shall reap

An Extraordinary Saint

in joy." "So was our mouth filled with laughter." But to let other men do all the painful sowing while he spent his whole time getting his idle sport out of their faults and foibles, like this big, playful champion of Israel, was not the way a strong man ought to live his life through, not good business for a saint.

Indeed, as we keep our eyes on this strange character, the wonder continually grows how any one ever ventured to call him a saint. What did Samson to deserve the title? "Through faith," says the Epistle to the Hebrews; but where did faith come in with a character like this?

That question was partly answered for us at the outset. This man was a Nazarite. "To touch no unclean thing, to drink no wine or strong drink, to leave his head unshaven"—so far as it went this was matter of religious principle with him, for he believed these peculiar customs to be God's will for him. His obedience in that one particular was matter of faith; that was not a jest. Samson laughed at almost everything else,

One Thread of Faith

but not at his own extraordinary head of hair; and I fancy if any unwary Philistine ever laughed at it in his presence, it was his last laugh in this world.

There does not seem much piety in that —that little patch of solemn reality in a man's life, when all the rest was treated so slightingly. No, it was very little; yet see how even that little may be enough to save the man. If a man's heart is bound to the holy will of God by any frailest bond of willing obedience, just that may be enough yet to save the man, that is, to let God save him. All the rest of Samson's life was somewhat ignoble; not deliberately wicked, perhaps, rude and undeveloped rather; a big, playful animal, too idle to lift himself to the dignity of moral choice. But here in the matter of his Nazarite vow was one moral principle, one thread of religious faith binding his big brute nature to the holy God above him; and while that thread holds, though the whole man may seem more animal than angel, yet there is hope of his final salvation.

An Extraordinary Saint

But let Samson beware how he ever lets that one frail thread be broken. A holier man, like Moses, touching God on every side, if he had chanced to be a long-haired Nazarite and some day had lost his hair, it might not have mattered much. But poor Samson, losing that hair of his, will have lost all the religion he ever had; the Lord was departed from him, his strength was turned to weakness.

You will see people who do not impress you as very godly, and yet you do believe them loyal to some principle; careless about other things, they have been faithful to that. Now I am glad to believe that any such faithfully cherished principle, which a man would not betray at any cost, may be a sort of germinal but genuine faith binding his soul to God.

But what if now the man should lose even that frail tie between his soul and heaven? Thank God if there is any one conviction or principle which in all the trials of life you have always held fast, never letting it go.

His Sin

Ah, but what if you should let it go now? If this Samson should wilfully break away from God by cutting off his own hair, that might really be for him what the New Testament calls the sin against the Holy Ghost.

You notice Samson was not guilty of that sin, not quite. He did not wilfully break his own vow; he did not cut off his own hair. His fault was in trusting a fair and false Philistine, letting her beguile his judgment till he told her all that was in his heart. That was fall enough for an Israelite. You have no right to give your whole heart so unreservedly to any Philistine, or any one else except the holy Lord above you. And the fault brought its swift and terrible penalty. The treacherous temptress betrayed him, of course, robbed him of his locks in his sleep and gave him to his enemies. They put out his eyes, and bound him with fetters of brass, and made him grind in their prison-house. At first view one would think the end of this man as disastrous as if with his own hand, with daring impiety, the Nazarite

An Extraordinary Saint

had shorn himself. So it often seems to us; the heedless faults of men seem to entail as fearful retribution as their deliberate crimes. The boy or man or woman overmastered by sudden temptation has let slip purity, honor, truth, integrity, and the life seems as utterly shipwrecked and darkened as if the sin had been committed with deliberate malice.

But it was not so; that is not the end of the story of this man. For it reads: "Howbeit the hair of his head began to grow again after he was shaven." I am not curious to mark out the precise line between history and poetic allegory in sentences so sublime as these. The divine favor and strength were not yet utterly forfeited for Samson; that is what we can understand. Even in his blindness the Spirit of God could begin to make him strong again. Why, that old scene in the dark Philistine prison-house glows with light as a prophecy of Christ's salvation. Have hope in God, you who have been betrayed and ruined by sin. There is hope in God for all, however lost, who truly repent

His Restoration

of their sin. For we know that God has sent One into the world, "and anointed him to preach deliverance to the captives, and recovering of sight to the blind, to set at liberty them that are bruised." That is the gospel of Christ: hope for the penitent, a glorious light that was not yet shining in those savage days of the judges; but can you not see a dim prophecy of it when you read, " Howbeit the hair of his head began to grow again after he was shaven"?

And so the lords of the Philistines are gathered to offer sacrifice in the temple of their god; and they send for their dishonored enemy to make sport for them; and his hands touched the pillars of the house, and one earnest prayer of faith rises to the God of his strength, and he bowed himself with all his might; and the epitaph stands: "The dead which he slew at his death were more than they which he slew in his life." So he died triumphantly at last, this Hebrew champion. He could be counted among the victorious believers, and his name will yet cheer his people to stubborn resistance and final victory over their Philistine oppressors; for God had regarded his penitence, the hair of his head grew and his strength came back to him in the prison.

Oh yes, we may have hope in God, however we may have been betrayed by the deceitfulness of sin.

Yet it was a sad and tragical triumph, after all—better than nothing; and if you were speaking to a company of miserable old men, who had already thrown away the chances and hopes of a lifetime, you would be glad to hold out to them even that sort of meager encouragement. Better to be saved so as by fire than to be lost altogether.

But I could not possibly satisfy myself with the thought of any such destiny for you— you men with the choice opportunities of life still looking you in the face. I chose this as a topic mainly with the purpose of urging you not to throw away your lives as that strong man threw away so much of his through his idle, aimless uselessness. Oh,

Walk in the Spirit

be sure to find some man's work to do; pray God to give you some man's work to do with your strength of body, and your strength of mind, and the natural, good-humored hopefulness of your young manhood. That is a prayer you need not fear to offer in Christ's name; it is a Christian prayer. If God will put enough strong, positive Christian purpose into your heart and life you will be safe from the Philistines, I think; but in no other way. If you are walking in the Spirit you will not fulfil the lusts of the flesh.

The Meaning of Manhood

By

Henry van Dyke, D.D.
Pastor of the Brick Church, New York

"How much, then, is a man better than a sheep!"—Matt. xii. 12.

ON the lips of Christ these noble words were an exclamation. He knew, as no one else has ever known, "what was in man." But to us who repeat them they often seem like a question. We are so ignorant of the deepest meaning of manhood, that we find ourselves at the point to ask in perplexity, How much, after all, is a man better than a sheep?

It is evident that the answer to this question must depend upon our general view of life. There are two very common ways of looking at existence that settle our judgment

The View of Materialism

of the comparative value of a man and a sheep, at once and inevitably.

Suppose, in the first place, that we take a materialistic view of life. Looking at the world from this standpoint, we shall see in it a great mass of matter, curiously regulated by laws which have results, but no purposes, and agitated into various modes of motion by a secret force whose origin is, and forever must be, unknown. Life, in man as in other animals, is but one form of this force. Rising through many subtle gradations, from the first tremor that passes through the gastric nerve of a jellyfish to the most delicate vibration of gray matter in the brain of a Plato or a Shakespeare, it is really the same from the beginning to the end—physical in its birth among the kindred forces of heat and electricity, physical in its death in cold ashes and dust. The only difference between man and the other animals is a difference of degree. The ape takes his place in our ancestral tree, and the sheep becomes our distant cousin.

It is true that we have somewhat the ad-

The Meaning of Manhood

vantage of these poor relations. We belong to the more fortunate branch of the family, and have entered upon an inheritance considerably enlarged by the extinction of collateral branches. But, after all, it is the same inheritance, and there is nothing in humanity which is not derived from and destined to our mother earth.

If, then, we accept this view of life, what answer can we give to the question, How much is a man better than a sheep? We must say: He is a little better, but not much. In some things he has the advantage. He lives longer, and has more powers of action and capacities of pleasure. He is more clever, and has succeeded in making the sheep subject to his domination. But the balance is not all on one side. The sheep has fewer pains as well as fewer pleasures, less care as well as less power. If it does not know how to make a coat, at least it succeeds in growing its own natural wool clothing, and that without taxation. Above all, the sheep is not troubled with any of those

The View of Commercialism

vain dreams of moral responsibility and future life which are the cause of such great and needless trouble to humanity. The flocks that fed in the pastures of Bethlehem got just as much physical happiness out of existence as the shepherd David who watched them, and, being natural agnostics, they were free from David's delusions in regard to religion. They could give all their attention to eating, drinking, and sleeping, which is the chief end of life. From the materialistic standpoint, a man may be a little better than a sheep, but not much.

Or suppose, in the second place, that we take the commercial view of life. We shall then say that all things must be measured by their money value, and that it is neither profitable nor necessary to inquire into their real nature or their essential worth. Men and sheep are worth what they will bring in the open market, and this depends upon the supply and demand. Sheep of a very rare breed have been sold for as much as five or six thousand dollars. But men of common

The Meaning of Manhood

stock, in places where men are plenty and cheap (as, for example, in Central Africa), may be purchased for the price of a rusty musket or a piece of cotton cloth. According to this principle, we must admit that the comparative value of a man and a sheep fluctuates with the market, and that there are times when the dumb animal is much the more valuable of the two.

This view, carried out to its logical conclusion, led to slavery, and put up men and sheep at auction on the same block, to be disposed of to the highest bidder. We have gotten rid of the logical conclusion. But have we gotten rid entirely of the premise on which it rested? Does not the commercial view of life still prevail in civilized society?

There is a certain friend of mine who often entertains me with an account of the banquets which he has attended. On one occasion he told me that two great railroads and the major part of all the sugar and oil in the United States sat down at the same table with three gold-mines and a line of steamships.

The Money Standard

"How much is that man worth?" asks the curious inquirer. "That man," answers some walking business directory, "is worth a million dollars; and the man sitting next to him is not worth a penny." What other answer can be given by one who judges everything by a money standard? If wealth is really the measure of value, if the end of life is the production or the acquisition of riches, then humanity must take its place in the sliding scale of commodities. Its value is not fixed and certain. It depends upon accidents of trade. We must learn to look upon ourselves and our fellowmen purely from a business point of view and to ask only: What can this man make? how much has that man made? how much can I get out of this man's labor? how much will that man pay for my services? Those little children that play in the squalid city streets —they are nothing to me or to the world; there are too many of them; they are worthless. Those long-fleeced, high-bred sheep that feed upon my pastures—they are among my most costly possessions; they will bring an enormous price; they are immensely valuable. How much is a man better than a sheep? What a foolish question! Sometimes the man is better; sometimes the sheep is better. It all depends upon the supply and demand.

Now these two views of life, the materialistic and the commercial, always have prevailed in the world. Men have held them consciously and unconsciously. At this very day there are some who profess them, and there are many who act upon them, although they may not be willing to acknowledge them. They have been the parents of countless errors in philosophy and sociology; they have bred innumerable and loathsome vices and shames and cruelties and oppressions in the human race. It was to shatter and destroy these falsehoods, to sweep them away from the mind and heart of humanity, that Jesus Christ came into the world. We cannot receive his gospel in any sense, we cannot begin to understand its scope and purpose, unless we fully, freely,

Christ Reveals Man to Himself

and sincerely accept his great revelation of the true meaning and value of man as man.

We say this was his revelation. Undoubtedly it is true that Christ came to reveal God to man. But undoubtedly it is just as true that he came to reveal man to himself. He called himself the Son of God, but he called himself also the Son of man. His nature was truly divine, but his nature was no less truly human. He became man. And what is the meaning of that lowly birth, in the most helpless form of infancy, if it be not to teach us that humanity is so related to deity that it is capable of receiving and embodying God himself? He died for man. And what is the meaning of that sacrifice, if it be not to teach us that God counts no price too great to pay for the redemption of the human soul? This gospel of our Lord and Saviour Jesus Christ contains the highest, grandest, most ennobling doctrine of humanity that ever has been proclaimed on earth. It is the only certain cure for low and debasing views of life. It is the only doctrine from which we

The Meaning of Manhood

can learn to think of ourselves and our fellow-men as we ought to think. I ask you to consider for a little while the teachings of Jesus Christ in regard to what it means to be a man.

Suppose, then, that we come to him with this question: How much is a man better than a sheep? He will tell us that a man is infinitely better, because he is the child of God, because he is capable of fellowship with God, and because he is made for an immortal life. And this threefold answer will shine out for us not only in the words, but also in the deeds, and above all in the death, of the Son of God and the Son of man.

1. Think, first of all, of the meaning of manhood in the light of the truth that man is the offspring and likeness of God. This was not a new doctrine first proclaimed by Christ. It was clearly taught in the magnificent imagery of the Book of Genesis. The chief design of that great picture of the beginnings is to show that a personal Creator is the source and author of all things

In the Image of God

that are made. But next to that, and of equal importance, is the design to show that man is incalculably superior to all the other works of God—that the distance between him and the lower animals is not a difference in degree, but a difference in kind. Yes, the difference is so great that we must use a new word to describe the origin of humanity, and if we speak of the stars and the earth, the trees and the flowers, the fishes, the birds, and the beasts, as "the works" of God, when man appears we must find a nobler name and say, "This is more than God's work; he is God's child."

Our human consciousness confirms this testimony and answers to it. We know that there is something in us which raises us infinitely above the things that we see and hear and touch, and the creatures that appear to spend their brief life in the automatic workings of sense and instinct. These powers of reason and affection and conscience, and above all this wonderful power of free will, the faculty of swift, sovereign, voluntary

The Meaning of Manhood

choice, belong to a higher being. We say not to corruption, "Thou art my father," nor to the worm, "Thou art my mother"; but to God, "Thou art my Father," and to the great Spirit, "In thee was my life born."

> "Not only cunning casts in clay:
> Let Science prove we are, and then
> What matters Science unto men,
> At least to me? I would not stay.
>
> "Let him, the wiser man who springs
> Hereafter, up from childhood shape
> His action like the greater ape;
> But I was *born* to other things."

Frail as our physical existence may be, in some respects the most frail, the most defenseless among animals, we are yet conscious of something that lifts us up and makes us supreme. "Man," says Pascal, "is but a reed, the feeblest thing in nature; but he is a reed that thinks. It needs not that the universe arm itself to crush him. An exhalation, a drop of water, suffice to destroy him. But were the universe to crush him, man is yet nobler than the universe; for he knows that he dies, and the universe, even in prevailing against him, knows not its power."

The Direct Appeal

Now the beauty and strength of Christ's doctrine of man lie, not in the fact that he was at pains to explain and defend and justify this view of human nature, but in the fact that he assumed it with an unshaken conviction of its truth, and acted upon it always and everywhere. He spoke to man, not as the product of nature, but as the child of God. He took it for granted that we are different from plants and animals, and that we are conscious of the difference. "Consider the lilies," he says to us; "the lilies cannot consider themselves: they know not what they are, nor what their life means; but you know, and you can draw the lesson of their lower beauty into your higher life. Regard the birds of the air; they are dumb and unconscious dependents upon the divine bounty, but you are conscious objects of the divine care. Are you not of more value than many sparrows?" Through all his words we feel the thrilling power of this high doctrine of humanity. He is always appealing to reason, to conscience, to the power of choice between good and evil, to the noble and godlike faculties in man.

And now think for a moment of the fact that his life was voluntarily, and of set purpose, spent among the poorest and humblest of mankind. Remember that he spoke, not to philosophers and scholars, but to peasants and fishermen and the little children of the world. What did he mean by that? Surely it was to teach us that this doctrine of the meaning of manhood applies to man as man. It is not based upon considerations of wealth or learning or culture or eloquence. Those are the things of which the world takes account, and without which it refuses to pay any attention to us. A mere man, in the eyes of the world, is a nobody. But Christ comes to humanity in its poverty, in its ignorance, stripped of all outward signs of power, destitute of all save that which belongs in common to mankind; to this lowly child, this very beggar-maid of human nature, comes the King, and speaks to her as a princess in disguise, and lifts her up and sets a crown upon

The Capacity of Fellowship

her head. I ask you if this simple fact ought not to teach us how much a man is better than a sheep.

2. But Christ reveals to us another and a still higher element of the meaning of manhood by speaking to us as beings who are capable of holding communion with God and reflecting the divine holiness in our hearts and lives. And here also his doctrine gains clearness and force when we bring it into close connection with his conduct. I suppose that there are few of us who would not be ready to admit at once that there are some men and women who have high spiritual capacities. For them, we say, religion is a possible thing. They can attain to the knowledge of God and fellowship with him. They can pray, and sing praises, and do holy work. It is easy for them to be good. They are born good. They are saints by nature. But for the great mass of the human race this is out of the question, absurd, impossible. They must dwell in ignorance, in wickedness, in impiety.

But to all this Christ says, "No!" No,

The Meaning of Manhood

to our theory of perfection for the few. No, to our theory of hopeless degradation for the many. He takes his way straight to the outcasts of the world, the publicans and the harlots and sinners, and to them he speaks of the mercy and the love of God and the beauty of the heavenly life; not to cast them into black despair, not because it was impossible for them to be good and to find God, but because it was divinely possible. God was waiting for them, and something in them was waiting for God. They were lost. But surely they never could have been lost unless they had first of all belonged to God, and this made it possible for them to be found again. They were prodigals. But surely the prodigal is also a child, and there is a place for him in the father's house. He may dwell among the swine, but he is not one of them. He is capable of remembering his father's love. He is capable of answering his father's embrace. He is capable of dwelling in his father's house in filial love and obedience.

That is the doctrine of Christ in regard to

The Lost Likeness

fallen and disordered and guilty human nature. It is fallen, it is disordered, it is guilty; but the capacity of reconciliation, of holiness, of love to God, still dwells in it, and may be quickened into a new life. That is God's work, but God himself could not do it if man were not capable of it.

Do you remember the story of the portrait of Dante which is painted upon the walls of the Bargello, at Florence? For many years it was supposed that the picture had utterly perished. Men had heard of it, but no one living had ever seen it. But presently came an artist who was determined to find it again. He went into the place where tradition said that it had been painted. The room was used as a storehouse for lumber and straw. The walls were covered with dirty whitewash. He had the heaps of rubbish carried away. Patiently and carefully he removed the whitewash from the wall. Lines and colors long hidden began to appear; and at last the grave, lofty, noble face of the great poet looked out again upon the world of light.

The Meaning of Manhood

"That was wonderful," you say, "that was beautiful!" Not half so wonderful as the work which Christ came to do in the heart of man—to restore the forgotten likeness of God and bring the divine image to the light. He comes to us with the knowledge that God's image is there, though concealed; he touches us with the faith that the likeness can be restored. To have upon our hearts the impress of the divine nature, to know that there is no human being in whom that treasure is not hidden and from whose stained and dusty soul Christ cannot bring out that reflection of God's face—that, indeed, is to know the meaning of manhood, and to be sure that a man is better than a sheep!

3. There is yet one more element in Christ's teaching in regard to the meaning of manhood, and that is his doctrine of immortality. This truth springs inevitably out of his teaching in regard to the origin and capacity of human nature. A being formed in the divine image, a being capable of reflecting the divine holiness, is a being so lofty

Immortality Brought to Light

that he must have also the capacity of entering into a life which is spiritual and eternal, and which leads onward to perfection. All that Christ teaches about man, all that Christ offers to do for man, opens before him a vast and boundless future.

This idea of immortality runs through everything that Jesus says and does. Never for a moment does he speak to man as a creature who is bound to this present world. Never for a moment does he forget, or suffer us to forget, that our largest and most precious treasures may be laid up in the world to come. He would arouse our souls to perceive and contemplate the immense issues of life.

The perils that beset us here through sin are not brief and momentary dangers, possibilities of disgrace in the eyes of men, of suffering such limited pain as our bodies can endure in the disintegrating process of disease, of dying a temporal death, which at the worst can only cause us a few hours of anguish. A man might bear these things, and take the risk of this world's shame and sickness

The Meaning of Manhood

and death, for the sake of some darling sin. But the truth that flashes on us like lightning from the word of Christ is that the consequence of sin is the peril of losing our immortality. "Fear not them which kill the body," said he, "but are not able to kill the soul; but rather fear him which is able to destroy both soul and body in hell."

On the other hand, the opportunities that come to us here through the grace of God are not merely opportunities of temporal peace and happiness. They are chances of securing endless and immeasurable felicity, wealth that can never be counted or lost, peace that the world can neither give nor take away. We must understand that now the kingdom of God has come near unto us. It is a time when the doors of heaven are open. We may gain an inheritance incorruptible, and undefiled, and that fadeth not away. We may lay hold not only on a present joy of holiness, but on an everlasting life with God.

It is thus that Christ looks upon the children of men: not as herds of dumb, driven cattle,

Our Need of Christ's Teaching

but as living souls moving onward to eternity. It is thus that he dies for men: not to deliver them from brief sorrows, but to save them from final loss and to bring them into bliss that knows no end. It is thus that he speaks to us, in solemn words before which our dreams of earthly pleasure and power and fame and wealth are dissipated like unsubstantial vapors: "What shall it profit a man, if he gain the whole world, and lose his own soul? Or what shall a man give in exchange for his soul?"

There never was a time in which Christ's doctrine of the meaning of manhood was more needed than it is to-day. There is no truth more important and necessary for us to take into our hearts, and hold fast, and carry out in our lives. For here we stand in an age when the very throng and pressure and superfluity of human life lead us to set a low estimate upon its value. The air we breathe is heavy with materialism and commercialism. The lowest and most debas-

The Meaning of Manhood

ing views of human nature are freely proclaimed and unconsciously accepted. There is no escape, no safety for us, save in coming back to Christ and learning from him that man is the child of God, made in the divine image, capable of the divine fellowship, and destined to an immortal life. I want to tell you just three of the practical reasons why we must learn this.

1. We need to learn it in order to understand the real meaning, and guilt, and danger, and hatefulness of sin.

Men are telling us nowadays that there is no such thing as sin. It is a dream, a delusion. It must be left out of account. All the evils in the world are natural and inevitable. They are simply the secretions of human nature. There is no more shame or guilt connected with them than with the malaria of the swamp or the poison of the nightshade.

But Christ tells us that sin is real, and that it is the enemy, the curse, the destroyer of mankind. It is not a part of man as God made him; it is a part of man as he has un-

How to Hate Sin

made and degraded himself. It is the marring of the divine image, the ruin of the glorious temple, the self-mutilation and suicide of the immortal soul. It is sin that casts man down into the mire. It is sin that drags him from the fellowship of God into the company of beasts. It is sin that leads him into the far country of famine, and leaves him among the swine, and makes him fain to fill his belly with the husks that the swine do eat. Therefore we must hate sin, and fear it, and abhor it, always and everywhere. When we look into our own heart and find sin there, we must humble ourselves before God and repent in sackcloth and ashes. Every sin that whispers in our heart is an echo of the world's despair and misery. Every selfish desire that lies in our soul is a seed of that which has brought forth strife, and cruelty, and murder, and horrible torture, and bloody war among the children of men. Every lustful thought that defiles our imagination is an image of that which has begotten loathsome vices and crawling shames throughout the world. My brother-men, God hates sin because it ruins man. And when we know what that means, when we feel that same poison of evil within us, we must hate sin as he does, and bow in penitence before him, crying, "God, be merciful to me a sinner."

2. We need to learn Christ's doctrine of the meaning of manhood in order to help us to love our fellow-men.

This is a thing that is easy to profess, but hard, bitterly hard, to do. The faults and follies of human nature are apparent. The unlovely and contemptible and offensive qualities of many people thrust themselves sharply upon our notice and repel us. We are tempted to shrink back, wounded and disappointed, and to relapse into a life that is governed by disgusts. If we dwell in the atmosphere of a Christless world, if we read only those newspapers which chronicle the crimes and meannesses of men, or those realistic novels which deal with the secret vices and corruptions of humanity, and fill our souls with the unspoken conviction that virtue is an old-

How to Love Men

fashioned dream, and that there is no man good, no woman pure, I do not see how we can help despising and hating mankind. Who shall deliver us from this spirit of bitterness? Who shall take us by the hand and lead us out of this heavy, fetid air of the lazar-house and the morgue?

None but Christ. If we will go with him, he will teach us not to hate our fellow-men for what they are, but to love them for what they may become. He will teach us to look, not for the evil which is manifest, but for the good which is hidden. He will teach us not to despair, but to hope, even for the most degraded of mankind. And so, perchance, as we keep company with him, we shall learn the secret of that divine charity which fills the heart with peace and joy and quiet strength. We shall learn to do good unto all men as we have opportunity, not for the sake of gratitude or reward, but because they are the children of our Father and the brethren of our Saviour. We shall learn the meaning of that blessed death on Calvary, and be willing

The Meaning of Manhood

to give ourselves as a sacrifice for others, knowing that he that turneth a sinner from the error of his ways shall save a soul from death and cover a multitude of sins.

3. Finally, we need to accept and believe Christ's doctrine of the meaning of manhood in order that it may lead us personally to God and a higher life.

You are infinitely better and more precious than the dumb beasts. You know it, you feel it; you are conscious that you belong to another world. And yet it may be that there are times when you forget it and live as if there were no God, no soul, no future life. Your ambitions are fixed upon the wealth that corrodes, the fame that fades. Your desires are toward the pleasures that pall upon the senses. You are bartering immortal treasure for the things which perish in the using. You are ignoring and despising the high meaning of your manhood. Who shall remind you of it, who shall bring you back to yourself, who shall lift you up to the level of your true being, unless it be the Teacher who spake as never man spake, the Master who brought life and immortality to light?

Come, then, to Christ, who alone can save you from the sin that defiles and destroys your manhood. Come, then, to Christ, who alone can make you good men and true, living in the power of an endless life. Come, then, to Christ, that you may have fellowship with him and realize all that it means to be a man.

Strength and Courage

By

Lewis O. Brastow, D.D.

Professor of Homiletics and the Pastoral Charge, Yale Divinity School

"Be strong and of a good courage."—Deut. xxxi. 6.

STRENGTH and courage are inseparable, and the injunction to be strong is nearly equivalent to the injunction to be courageous. "Be strong" can only mean "Rally the strength you have." "Be courageous" means "Concentrate your strength against danger or difficulty." Courage, then, is the application of manly force in confronting obstacles. Courage is strong-heartedness. Etymologically it suggests that the heart is the innermost center, "the rallying-ground," of the forces of moral manhood. Of one who does not or cannot rally his resources of strength we say that he is discouraged, dis-

Rational Faith

heartened, has lost heart. We are dealing, therefore, with a rational rather than with an animal quality. It is a virtue in so far as it involves a rational, self-determined effort in confronting the contradictions of life. It is a quality of character rather than a condition of nerve or muscle. It is of this courage that I wish to speak. It is the courage of intelligence and freedom, the courage of self-determined moral purpose, the courage of moral strength, and it has many forms. Their ethical quality is conditioned by the influences that produce them, or by the principles that enter into them and the motive forces that dominate them. The courage inculcated by my text would of course take the form of a Hebrew virtue. But I wish to transfer this injunction to the realm of Christian morality and to speak of the more specifically Christian forms of that moral strength which involves moral courage.

1. Such courage is preëminently the courage of a rational faith. In every struggle, physical, political, moral, whatever it may be,

Strength and Courage

a man needs good footing. It is an athlete's first necessity to look out for his feet. The moral athlete who makes a successful stand against the difficulties of life must have good standing-ground. Faith gives us footing. Skepticism is a sapper and miner. It takes the ground from under our feet. A man must feel that he has something under him, something he can trust. Difficulty brings one to a stand, throws him back upon some resource. Courage is the girding of strength for resistance. It is will rallying the dormant or scattered forces of manhood to conflict. The rally must be made from the basis of something to which one is self-committed in mental and moral confidence. One must know that he stands on something that he can trust. In any difficulty or danger the mind must be in a positive attitude of confidence. No man can fight difficulties in the air. There is nothing but moral imbecility in perpetual distrust or doubt. It is not religion alone, but morality, nor yet morality also, but the want of life and the make of the

The Vantage-ground of Faith

soul, that demands faith. An over-skeptical habit of mind involves moral paralysis. In any difficulty one sees as never otherwise how necessary it is to believe in something, to believe in it positively and energetically and even in spite of one's self and despite all compromising appearances. Faith is vantage-ground for the battle. It is the Round Top, the key-point of the situation for the battle of life. A man may find a certain standing-ground in himself. Well, God has put strength into manhood, and he gives men ample opportunity to test it, and a man ought to be able to believe in himself. To distrust one's self in a pinch is to invite defeat. It is not safe to suspend one's self in the uncertainty of self-distrust. One must trust other men also. No one can stand alone. We are obliged to believe in our fellow-men. A man must also trust the world in which he lives, and above all the God who is over it and in it. In other words, the courage of all soundest moral strength centers in faith, in a higher power above us, and in the moral

Strength and Courage

order of the world. A surrender of faith in God and Providence would leave the world in the imbecility of despair. And I question if there be not in all rational faith in personal manhood, in fellow-men, and in the world in which we live a certain latent or implicit confidence in a higher power and in a moral order that has a rational and moral beginning and goal. Certain it is that when men begin to think ethically and rationally they are obliged to postulate the reality of God as a basis of confidence in the ultimate victory of life. This courage of faith in God is the old Hebrew courage. The courage of self-confidence is no Hebrew virtue. That would be disloyalty to God. To be strong is to be strong in God. It is the God of the fathers, the covenant God, that is committed to them and will see them through. And the one great central virtue of Hebrew ethics was faith in a covenant God.

The same stress is put upon faith in the ethics of the Christian life. And this is no insignificant thing as related to the moral con-

Faith in Redemption

flict of life. Faith is a fundamental virtue in the battle of life, because it is only unto faith that we shall add a manly courage. This conception of a Father God who would make us his own possession, would hold us in fellowship with himself, would throw about us the shield of his loving protection and carry us victoriously through into the crown-heights of our redemption, is ever struggling into view in all prophetic Scriptures, and it breaks forth in all its completeness and magnificence in the revelation of God as the Father of our Lord Jesus Christ. It is the God of redemption that is committed to us and will see us through the struggle of life. The greater includes the lesser good. "He that spared not his own Son, but delivered him up for us all, how shall he not also with him freely give us all things?" is the word of lofty cheer. Christian courage, then, is the courage of faith in the calling of redemption as the divine calling of life.

2. It is the courage of rational moral conviction. Conviction involves the action of

Strength and Courage

truth in the conscience. It gets lodged there in the way of moral conquest. Moral truth is well intrenched only when it is intrenched in an intelligent conscience, and the only valiant soldier in its army is the man who carries it about with him in his moral conviction as a man carries his life and force in the blood of his heart. The man who is morally mastered by the truth is himself masterful. To be thus morally vanquished in the domain of truth and held in allegiance to it is to be a conqueror in its service. It is a dangerous thing for the evil of this world when the truth gets intrenched in the moral sense. It is not enough that it carry a man's intelligence. Moral realities do not get very deep root in the soil of the mind alone. Convince and persuade a man, and he may not remain convinced or persuaded. The truth must get below the mind and below emotion, that only transiently dominates the will. But it has won a great victory when it gets hold of the conscience and wins men to its intelligent service. It makes valiant men

The Vitality of Moral Conviction

of them. When a man invests with moral sacredness what he holds for truth he will maintain it against all comers and will advance with it in the face of all opposition. Men do not sacrifice much for nor stand by what they hold indifferently. They stand for the truth only when it takes vital hold of them. It is a respectable thing to think correctly, and indeed it is a safe thing to hold correct theories, for they are likely to work themselves out in practical life. But the quality of correctness is not enough. Living things hold by the root, and they need good soil. Rational moral soil is the only soil that is fit for the truth one holds with tenacity and defends with courage. He who turns his back upon what he professes to believe and honor, and plays the coward, demonstrates that it has taken but little hold of the vital part of him. We in this easy-going age demonstrate that we have lost all genuine sympathy with the men of better days,—days of martyr spirits, days of supremest moral grandeur,—have lost capacity for courageous and heroic moral witnessing, in so far as we permit the most vital and commanding truths and realities of human life to become open questions and play fast and loose in our allegiance to them. The passive virtue of humility is indeed a Christian virtue, but it is a humility that should be matched by the most heroic and aggressive boldness. We hear much in the New Testament about boldness. That was a brave church, that apostolic church. This boldness took the form of free and open utterance and of action corresponding. It was the boldness that says it all out freely, fully, uncompromisingly, without fear or favor, whether men will hear or forbear, and whatever the issue, as from God's inspiration. To say what was in them and to act from the inner stress of conviction was simply to obey God. They did not stop to balance dangers against duties. They spoke and acted and took the consequences, and they won a victory unmatched in human history. It was not temporizing, it was not political trimming, it was not partizan cowardice, that founded

Moral Force Rules the World

Christianity. Nor is it that sort of moral imbecility that shall perpetuate it. Christian men will never be influential, they will never be respectable, without moral strength. Strength is what this world is looking for and what it is sure to respect. It is moral strength that is bound to rule this world, and it is what the world needs to-day. There is a loud call to-day for the pluck of old-fashioned manly men. Before the political Pontius Pilates of our age we need living witnesses of Him who, in the presence of their great prototype, witnessed his good confession: " To this end was I born, and for this cause came I into the world, that I might bear witness to the truth." The world will never be won to righteousness by surrendering at discretion to its dominant spirit. The moral conqueror of this world should not be sacrificed to it by those who undertake to represent him. Christ does not know the man, and will repudiate him, who sacrifices him and his cause to his old enemy. Above the iron doors of an " ample house " spoken of in

Strength and Courage

Spenser's "Faerie Queene" stand three inscriptions. Over the first the words "Be bold." Over the second, "much fayrer than the former, and richlier," was "likewise writ, 'Be bold, be bold, and everywhere be bold.'" And on the third, "Be not too bold." The iron doorways these of a mysterious and treacherous life. Longfellow in his "Morituri Salutamus" has wrought these inscriptions and left them as a fit battle-call to the young men of this congregation and of the nation:

> "Write on your doors the saying wise and old,
> 'Be bold, be bold, and everywhere be bold;
> But not too bold.' Yet better the excess
> Than the defect; better the more than less;
> Better like Hector on the field to die,
> Than like a perfumed Paris turn and fly."

Not too bold; not shallow audacity; the sober courage of strong moral conviction—this is Christian courage, and this is what the world needs to-day. What a man holds to be true and right let him hold firmly and courageously; let him be willing to fight for it. We want no half-hearted, half-souled, or

Devotion is Moral Concentration

double-minded religion. Away with a lackadaisical piety! Religion must be manly. If it tolerate moral imbecility it will not win respect. The man whose religion is strapped up by moral conviction will add to it the virtue of a manly courage.

3. A rational devotion also lies at the foundation of strong and courageous character. Devotion implies an object to be attained, upon which one concentrates his energies. There is a goal to be reached. It lies beyond all intervening obstacle, difficulty, or danger, and to reach it one concentrates effort upon it. Any sort of devotion, even the commonest, involves a rallying of one's personal forces about a central and commanding purpose to reach the desired object at all hazard and despite all difficulty. And here is the rallying-ground of courage. In fact, what is courage but devotion to a desired object in the face of all obstacles? The man in ordinary secular life who makes all struggle for the attainment of his object conditional upon the personal ease or comfort with which

Strength and Courage

he can do it, or who has no object at all that he is willing to put the other side of whatever difficulties may arise, and has no dominant purpose with respect to any supreme object whatever, is a moral imbecile; he is a man without moral life and character. A man may be thrown back and baffled and confused by some sudden stroke of calamity, but if he be a man his manhood will assert itself and he will clear away the barriers and start again. Imbecility in the presence of difficulty is moral cowardice. Think of a business or professional man or a student making the purpose of his life conditional upon getting on without loss, or upon having an easy time of it! He who puts his aim this side of all difficulty and surrenders when difficulty comes will not reach very far or very high in this world's affairs.

Now all concentrated and persistent effort in the work of life must rally about this central purpose, and this purpose will successfully meet all difficulty that lies scattered along the entire life-path. Such a life

The Personal Factor

must be a strong and courageous life. It is the life of one who puts the object of his striving far over and beyond the farthest mountain-peak of earthly difficulty and who has an inclusive and commanding purpose to go over, mastering every barrier till he compass the object of his life. This mighty purpose to reach the goal of life is a species of devotion. When the purpose is of supreme ethical importance it is religious devotion. But Christian devotion involves another factor, which in reality is its chief characteristic. It is the personal factor. It is the devotion of personal love and loyalty to Jesus Christ. The strength and courage of Christian devotion are more than a consecrated purpose to realize the ethical ends of the Christian life. It is a purpose that centers in personal love and allegiance to Him who is himself the source and the inspiration and the pattern and the end of all Christian life. He only can determine the objects for which his disciple may live. In him alone is the spring and the motive and the guidance

Strength and Courage

we need in reaching the object he sets before us, and the strength of devotion will depend on the personal relation. The aim of life can never be reached without love for personal beings. We know this in the experiences of common life. The moral life of the world is dependent on personal relations. Some form of piety is necessary to morality. It is preëminently true in the higher domain of religion. The constraint of Christ's love is the heart of Christian devotion. And what is Christian courage but the soul's trusting and loving self-preservation for the tasks of life, in face of all difficulty and obstacle and danger, out of a sentiment and principle of gratitude to Him who is of right the Lord and Master of life?

4. To a rational faith, conviction, and devotion there should be added a rational hope as the crown and completion of a strong and courageous Christian life. What we strive for must be attainable in some measure and form at least, or strength and courage fail. If hope should fail the battle of life would

The Genesis of Hope

end. All over the field men would drop and rise no more. The powers of manhood would fail, and the end would be a universal wail of despair. Nothing would remain but the abyss of ruin to demonstrate that life is poisoned fatally at the root, that the heart of the universe is evil, and that existence is a gigantic failure and mockery. Some fragment at least of the good of life we must reasonably hope to win. God put desire and strength and confidence into the soul of man for the battle of life. Desire of the good, or what seems the good, consciousness of personal strength and confidence in the universe without or in what lies under it, one or both —these are the elements of his equipment for the conflict, and out of these hope is born. You want the good as your portion; you believe in the force God has lodged in you with reference to its attainment; you believe in the world in which you live; or, better still, as crowning and completing all and as holding the key of all mystery, you believe in the God that made the world and set your life in

Strength and Courage

its environment. Therefore you hope, and therefore you have courage for the battle of life. And there is always an abundant stock of hope on hand for the world at large. All over the world we see its conquests. The heart of man in a struggling life is demonstration that good lies behind and before. It is God's witness. That it is possible amid life's mountain barriers is intimation that good is the law of life and good its final goal. It is the outreach of man's prophetic soul after the good that is obscured by the shadows of life and barred by its contradictions. It is mightier than all obstacles, brightening above the glare of consuming flames, buoying amid devouring floods, singing amid the groanings of the flesh, exalting itself in the faintings of sorrow, strong in infirmity, triumphing in defeat, and living in the agonies of death. What a world it is, and what a life is this human life! If this small fragment of it were the end, it sometimes seems as if no power of last defeat could crush the energies of this strange struggling creature, man. It is

The Song of Hope

clear enough that the world was built for conquest by him, even material conquest. But it was built, too, for moral conquest, and what we need is hope for moral conquest. To conquer the world is not to conquer the untrained forces of the soul, nor to conquer sin, nor to conquer death. We are conquering the material world in this nation of ours, but materialism and animalism and sordid selfishness are conquering us. But not all men are conquering in the battle of material life. The notes of discontent all about us are bodeful. They may portend the desolation of a coming tempest. Many give up the struggle. What shall we do with the baffled? After all, is it not the larger number with whom the world goes ill? And there is a little joyous section of this struggling world, weighted with the common sorrows, but joyful still, that for almost nineteen centuries has been singing the song of hope to keep the weary brotherhood and sisterhood in heart. The literature of hope is very rich. And it suggests how much the song of hope is

Strength and Courage

needed in the bafflings of life. How many a burdened heart and baffled life has sung out the hope that has been kindled at the altar-flame of a divine redemption unto the rallying of the weary and burdened and despairing brotherhood of the unblessed! The hope that is earth-born is not enough. The true goal of life is "where beyond these voices there is peace." We need a divine hand to tear away the darkness of life and disclose the crown that glitters for the conqueror amid the glories of the perfected kingdom of redemption. The song of the redemption hope is a new song for earth. It is this hope of eternal redemption that holds the soul to its heavenly inheritance. Courage for the moral conflict of life, courage to meet the power of sin and of the last great enemy, is the courage of Christian hope. The voice of the resurrection hope has been lifted in the darkness and suffering of earth. What Jesus Christ has done for the strength and courage of the world by his revelation of the hope of eternal life and its rewards for the weary

The Song of the Resurrection Hope

of earth no human intelligence can well estimate.

Share, young men, with this conqueror of sin and death his spoils of conquest, and share his assurances of the ultimate completion of that universal kingdom which is "righteousness, peace, and joy in the Holy Ghost."

The Peril of Protracted Temptation

By

Teunis S. Hamlin, D.D.
Pastor of the Church of the Covenant, Washington, D. C.

"Joab had turned after Adonijah, though he turned not after Absalom."—1 Kings ii. 28.

JOAB was David's nephew, the second of the three sons of his sister Zeruiah. His youngest brother, Asahel, famous for his swiftness in running, was killed by Abner at the battle of Gibeon. The oldest, Abishai, a brave, fierce, revengeful man, was always at his uncle's side and rendered him invaluable service. But Joab, greatest in military prowess, as well as most statesmanlike, reached the place of power next the king himself. He treacherously killed Abner, partly in revenge for his brother's death and partly lest he should hold under David the same post of

Joab's Greatness

commander-in-chief that he had held under Saul. The king was grieved and outraged at this act, and compelled Joab to attend Abner's funeral in sackcloth and with rent robe. Still, induced, no doubt, by his preëminent fitness, he gave him Abner's place. Joab had fairly won this by accepting the challenge of David to scale the rock of Jebus and thus capture the fortress that was to become the national capital. So far as defense and conquest are concerned he may be called the founder of the kingdom. He made his headquarters in Jerusalem and had a magnificent country residence near by. He enjoyed almost royal titles and honors. He was devotedly loyal to his uncle and master. At the siege of Rabbah he took the lower town on the river, and then sent for the king to come and capture the fortress, lest the glory of the victory should attach to the name of Joab. He boldly disobeyed orders in killing the king's rebel son, Absalom, and with equal boldness reproved the king for his frantic grief, recalled him to his duty to his subjects, and

The Peril of Protracted Temptation

constrained him to show himself in public. This was the more unmistakably an act of loyalty since he had brought about a reconciliation between father and son after the latter had murdered Amnon in revenge for the outrage upon his sister Tamar. He wickedly acquiesced in David's murderous scheme against Uriah, but openly opposed him in numbering the people. Superseded by Amasa, he treacherously killed his rival and recovered his old place. He died at last by violence, David on his death-bed having charged Solomon to avenge Abner and Amasa.

Such are the chief incidents of an active, stormy life, quite consonant with the general tenor of the times. We are not now concerned with it as biography, though it is very fascinating biography; nor as a miniature of the life of the day, though in that aspect it is most instructive. But it has a moral and spiritual lesson of great value.

Joab was loyal to his sovereign through a long life. He was loyal against many temptations to be otherwise. From the time of

Joab's Relations to David

Abner's death David feared his impetuous, passionate nephews; indeed, he said at the funeral, "I am this day weak, though anointed king; and these men the sons of Zeruiah are too hard for me."* Joab could not have been uninfluenced by this fact; it is difficult for an inferior to retain respect for a superior who he knows fears him, or whom he regards as in any essential particular a weaker man than himself. Moreover, he was in the secret of his master's great crime—guilty, indeed, as an accessory, but not so guilty as the principal, and so with another consciousness of superiority which worked against his devotion. And monarchy was new in Israel. The king reigned more by virtue of his personal power than of an established habit of obedience on the part of his people. There were the incessant intrigues against the throne that to this day mark all Oriental governments. A score of times Joab must have been solicited to join the fortunes of this or that pretender, to accept anything that he

* 2 Sam. iii. 39.

The Peril of Protracted Temptation

chose to ask, to escape the growing ill will of his sovereign and avenge the repeated slights that he had suffered. Against all solicitations he had stood firm year after year. But now David is near his end—in fact, is almost comatose. It is known that he has promised the succession to a younger son, Solomon. The legitimist party, who favor the oldest son, Adonijah, determine not to wait for the king's death, but to at once seize the throne. It is particularly odious treason against a dying and presumably helpless man. And it is especially pitiful to find the aged Joab engaged in it. A few years before he had resisted the pretensions of the fascinating and popular Absalom, and at the risk of his own life had put him to death, as he deserved. But meanwhile his moral fiber has deteriorated. He lacks the robust virtue of other years. Even the thought of his dying sovereign and of the great things that they had passed through together cannot hold him to loyalty. So he " turns after Adonijah, though he had not turned after Absalom."

Age Does Not Insure Safety

The theory is commonly held that old men and women are safe from temptation. We talk about character being formed, settled, fixed. We speak of unassailable virtue. We devote all our skill and energy to safeguarding the young, which is right; but we neglect to throw any protection about the middle-aged, which is wrong. We treat ourselves in the same fashion, assuming that, say, after middle life we are in small peril of going astray. We accordingly subject our virtues to strains to which we would not have thought of exposing them twenty or thirty years earlier. Hence every community is frequently shocked by acts of amazing folly, vice, and even crime on the part of those who were supposed to have outlived all temptation in such directions. Hence we have the proverb, "Count no man happy until he is dead"—until he has passed beyond the possibility of throwing away by one stupendous blunder or sin the accumulated good reputation of three- or fourscore years. We say of such a man, " He was old enough to know better," which is in effect a confession that knowing better by no means carries with it the strength to do better. Hamlet regards it as the gravamen of his mother's offense in her criminal marriage with the king that she had passed the age when she could plead the excuse of impetuous passions. History, literature, our own observation unite to demonstrate that, while youth is imperiled by temptation, age is not safe, and to give some countenance to the rather harsh maxim that "there is no fool like an old fool."

The fact is that the danger that lurks in temptation is not a matter of age at all. Personality is of course the main thing. We are tempted according to our heredity, our appetites, our constitutional or acquired weaknesses, our individual proclivities toward this or that sin. These vary at different periods of life. Hence some temptations are strongest in youth, others in maturity, others in old age. There is a sense, too, in which youth is weaker to resist than maturity or age. The

Physical Perils

moral fiber, like the physical, is not yet toughened. Physicians tell us that the period of greatest peril to life, after infancy, is from eighteen to twenty-five or thirty years. All vital organs have developed rapidly; one looks most robust; he will quickly take high physical training in any direction, and, if he endures it, gain marvelous power. But at the same time he lacks high efficiency to resist or throw off disease. Add to this such imprudence as must accompany the unthinking conviction that nothing can harm him,—that he may eat and sleep and exercise as irregularly as he pleases,—and it is not marvelous that so many young men die in their years of greatest promise and apparently highest vitality. They are carried off by disease before they have learned their own powers of endurance, or, knowing them, gained the moral courage to live well within them. It is not an irrational solicitude, therefore, that parents feel for the health of their sons and daughters even after they are old enough to be supposed to wisely care for themselves.

The Peril of Protracted Temptation

Here the moral and spiritual nature affords a close analogy to the physical. Time brings to the soul certain qualifications to resist temptation that nothing else can bring, such as an intelligent fear of doing wrong and an accurate conception of its pernicious consequences. Especially it brings the *habit* of resisting the wrong and doing the right. And it is to that settled habit more than to anything else, except the immediate grace of God, that we all owe our moral safety.

But if the young are thus specially exposed at some points, they are also specially safeguarded at others. Their generous openheartedness saves them from meanness, which is the essence of so many of the sins of later life. They largely lack that calculating selfishness which, in the fierce struggle for success in the world, lures to dishonesty and to all the schemes of cold-blooded, relentless ambition. In fact, they stand against temptation far more nobly than could be fairly expected. Some—indeed, too many—go down and make early shipwreck, or lay the

Joab Finally Yields

foundations of certain disaster in later years; but the vast majority stand and put to shame the fears of those who believe too little both in the essential integrity of human nature and in the environing grace of God.

But, whatever the age, the real peril of temptation lies in its being long continued. It was not because Joab was old that he turned after Adonijah, while a few years before he had not turned after Absalom, but because at that time the temptation of disloyalty to his king had not been long enough at work to undermine his powers of resistance. When, however, Adonijah raised the standard of revolt and invited Joab to join him, the soliciting voice had spoken so many times, and each time more alluringly, that his ability to say no had been exhausted. He threw away reputation, honor, life itself, not because he was a weak old man,—for he was not that,—but because he had exposed himself through a series of years to the temptation that he had always hitherto been able to master, but that now at last mastered him.

The Peril of Protracted Temptation

Judas seems to have been a younger man than Joab—probably had not reached middle life; but he was a weaker man morally. What David's general had endured for forty years, that Christ's disciple was not able to endure for three. From the time that he became treasurer of the little band we can see avarice soliciting him. The Lord seems to have carefully guarded him; for instance, in letting Peter, not Judas, pay the Temple tax. But his power of resistance was steadily decreasing as the coin clinked in the bag at his girdle. He had handled only small sums, and when thirty pieces of silver dazzled his fancy *he must have them*, though it meant the betrayal of his best friend. It was just another case of Joab "turning after Adonijah, though he had not turned after Absalom."

The fact is, dear friends,—and herein lies the reason for the young standing so grandly as they do,—that few are swept away by the first attack of temptation. The fortress of our instinctive love of the right and our careful early training is not usually carried by

Steel Gives Way at Last

assault, but by sapping and mining. Grant conquered Lee by steady and persistent pounding, in the spirit of the famous despatch, "I propose to fight it out on this line if it takes all summer." The bravest army ever marshaled—and none braver than Lee's ever took the field—cannot forever stand such dogged attacks from an enemy with resources sufficient to keep them up indefinitely. Nor can the strongest human nature stand such attacks of temptation. No matter how confident you and I are of the quality of our moral fiber, we will act unwisely in subjecting it to too prolonged a strain.

Indeed, this law holds throughout all nature. We speak, for instance, of the life of a steel rail, meaning the period during which it can do its work. The incessant hammering on it of locomotive and car wheels finally changes the relation of its molecules until their coherence is so weakened that the strength of the metal is gone. Suddenly there is an unaccountable railway accident. It means only that rail or bridge or locomo-

The Peril of Protracted Temptation

tive had been strained, not too hard, but too long. They stood through Absalom's day, but could not stand through Adonijah's.

There is in the Moyamensing prison an old man who had worked for forty-three years in the mint at Philadelphia. He had risen from the humblest place to be chief weigher—from being watched to watching others. He was esteemed incorruptible and implicitly trusted. He was not extravagant and had no vices. But suddenly it was found that he was stealing gold bullion. He was not selling it—was practically deriving no benefit from it; he was not taking gold coins, which were equally at his disposal, nor did he seem to want them; but the gold bars he could not resist. He had handled them year after year and under steadily decreasing danger of detection should he steal them; his moral fiber was insensibly weakened, as dry-rot weakens an oak beam; at last it broke, and he was a thief. It was not that he was handling more gold, or that any stress of circumstances impelled him. It was not that temptation was stronger, but

The Strongest Body Poisoned

that he was weaker. He "turned after Adonijah, though he had not turned after Absalom."

Bacteriologists say that the germs of many or most diseases exist in our bodies while we are in good health; but we are able to resist them. There comes a time, however, when such resistance is weakened by that clogging of the system that we call a cold, and we have pneumonia; or when our foes are reinforced by impure water, and we have typhoid fever. We can withstand for a long time—a marvelously long time—the poison of a foul atmosphere, but the most robust constitution will finally succumb to it. We are horrified by stories of plagues and pestilences, as the yellow fever, cholera, the black death. They sweep over a country with awful devastation. But they pass by, and, after all, do not kill one where bad ventilation and unsanitary drainage, with their endless persistence, kill ten. The mighty storms that sweep the Matterhorn throw down with awful crash only the rocks that the constantly trickling and

The Peril of Protracted Temptation

freezing rills of water have through years or centuries insensibly crowded to the edge of the cliff.

I feel sure, dear friends, that in determining our moral safety or peril we give far too little heed to this matter of protracted temptation. I say nothing now of the duty of employers to safeguard their employees by careful and constant oversight, or of the many other important social bearings of the matter, but I wish that we all might profoundly realize its relation to ourselves. If we do realize it we will avoid giving any temptation a long-continued chance to undermine our resistance. The vital question is not whether we are younger or older, but whether the solicitation of evil can reach us for a shorter or longer period. No doubt we can resist once, twice, a dozen times; but it is not so clear that we can resist twenty times or a hundred. One might think that, as Joab did not turn after the handsome, gallant, fascinating Absalom, he was safe from ever becoming a renegade. But no; he turned after Adonijah. We may

Perfect Safety in God

be too proud to believe that we who have withstood so long can ever yield, but this is the very "pride that goeth before destruction." "I do not allow myself to look at a bad picture," said Sir Peter Lely, the artist, "for if I do my brush is certain to take a hint from it." The only safe way to treat a temptation that has begun to meet us frequently is the way of this wise book: "Avoid it, pass not by it, turn from it, and pass on." And even this counsel, good as we at once recognize it to be, we will not heed unless we seek divine grace. And that is ready: "God is faithful, who will not suffer you to be tempted above that ye are able; but will with the temptation make also the way of escape, that ye may be able to endure it." Trust him and you shall not turn after either Absalom or Adonijah.

The Gospel's View of Our Life

By

Rev. Joseph H. Twichell

Pastor of the Asylum Hill Congregational Church, Hartford, Conn.

" Paul, an apostle (not from men, neither through man, but through Jesus Christ, and God the Father, who raised him from the dead), and all the brethren which are with me, unto the churches of Galatia: Grace to you and peace from God the Father, and our Lord Jesus Christ, who gave himself for our sins, that he might deliver us out of this present evil world, according to the will of our God and Father: to whom be the glory for ever and ever. Amen."
—*Gal. i. 1–5.*

THIS salutatory benediction, with the like of which St. Paul opens all his letters, pulsates with feeling—feeling transparently generated by thoughts and affections that move in the highest plane. By reference or by implication the characteristic truths, views, sentiments of the Christian religion are embraced in it. It would make a text for sermons on several subjects. But what just now

Penetrated with the Sense of its Greatness

I would note in it is the *sense of life and of life's meaning* to himself and to those to whom he is speaking which the apostle reveals in it—that general import as conveyed in the nature of the things it touches upon and in its tone. So taken it is as an opening by which we may look into his mind and mark in what lights the world and men habitually appear to him—the common world and common men. For we are to consider that he is addressing people who are nothing out of the ordinary. This letter of his, when it reaches its destination, will be read to congregations or companies, of tradesmen, artisans, laborers, and their families, come together on the Sabbath or in the evening after the day's work is over, probably in some private house. They are before him as he writes. It is to such that he deems a greeting of so exalted a strain, breathing the atmosphere of spiritual realities, reaching in scope to eternal horizons, not inappropriate but appropriate. Approaching them in that manner, he is not *above* the level, but *at* the level of their life as he con-

The Gospel's View of Our Life

ceives it; which is to say, he is affected with an idea of their life that makes it a wonderfully great thing to his thought, not as their life alone, but as human life. What we are observing is but the expression, in one form, of what has been fitly termed the Enthusiasm of Humanity that distinguished him. To him all men alike, as he contemplates them in the situation and experience of this mortality, are the subjects of an overpowering interest, sympathy, concern.

And in this he most truly represents the Christian gospel; for it is certainly a fundamental trait of it, stamped upon it by its Author, that to an incomparable degree it discerns and feels the element of magnitude in human life as such. It is pervaded by an intense emotion, the subject of which is man as it sees him and knows him in those earthly conditions that are universal. Because of that insight and knowledge it is kindled with the desire of entering into communication with his mind and spirit. It has somewhat to say to him that it is immensely eager to

Is Apt to Seem Overdrawn

say. And so it is part of our preparation to understand the suitableness of the gospel to man's needs, part of our preparation to hear it for ourselves, somehow to view life in a way to make us share its feeling about it—the feeling, i.e., of those features, accompaniments, contents of it that fill it in all circumstances with a profound import.

It may seem strange to say that in order to do this, in order justly to compute the facts of the life we are living and that is being lived all around us, it is necessary for us to pause and consider. But nothing is truer than that it is necessary; for of the really large ingredients of life—our own and that of others—we are in a manner unconscious, or much of the time unconscious. I mean we do not think of it in their light. We incline to estimate life by its inferior aspects. This is commonplace, but so it is. And when the gospel speaks its great words to us they strike us at first as unfitting to such an affair as life is with us and with our fellows. They seem pitched to too high a key.

The Gospel's View of Our Life

It is not, however, the gospel alone that beholds the scene with another eye. Take, for example, out of many I might name, such a book as Mr. Barrie's "Window in Thrums." Thrums is a village of Scotch weavers whose years are spent in task-work of the most drudging sort; whose dwellings, abutting on narrow, gloomy streets, are cheerless; whose backs are bent with toil; whose life-story, to the casual observer, and to themselves probably, were they to tell it, is from youth to age that of an unremitting struggle with poverty. But no, that is not their story at all; rather, it transpires, only the merest outside and framework of it. For as you sit at his window beside the writer, who has lived there, and listen to him while he relates what, in the exercise of his gift of penetrating sight, he has watched going on among those people in their homes, in their relations with one another, in their private annals, in their hearts,—the joys, the sorrows; the hopes, the fears; the loves, the enmities; the nobleness, the baseness; the moral victories, the

The Main Contents of Experience Veiled

moral defeats,—your sense of the dullness and paltriness of their lot gives place to the sense of its dramatic and tragic nature. There is material there for a Shakespeare to use, plenty of it. Nor is there anything in the Bible that overshoots the mark presented by that community. And it is so everywhere, in all communities. It is so here among you.

We are wont to speak of one's life as though it were principally summed up in his business, his occupation, his pursuit. But that is only an incident of his life. Much of his experience as may be connected with it, more—far more—is aside from it and is another story. You pass one another on the campus, each going about his occasions; you exchange greetings; your acquaintance is perhaps familiar, even intimate; you are considerably informed of one another's circumstances and happenings; yet how little you know of one another after all! Some things, indeed, that are among the causes of your classmate's cheer or trouble, that touch him deeply, you are aware of, and he has your

The Gospel's View of Our Life

sympathy accordingly. But in his soul are private chambers into which you do not see—neither you nor any one else, probably. And so there are in yours. We all wear masks behind which the multitude of the motions of our thoughts is veiled and hidden. And it is a happy thing that we do; for were it otherwise—were all, that from the natural instinct of reserve or for other reasons, we keep to ourselves, revealed—we could hardly go on transacting with one another as we do and as it is necessary we should. Every once in a while as pastor I come to the knowledge of, for instance, some cross, heavy, bitter, long borne in silence, unsuspected, betrayed by no sign; and when that occurs my view of the life concerned is changed, sometimes very greatly, and I seem then to be warned to go softly among my people, for I do not know how many things of that kind there are about me.

You to whom I am now speaking are a community of students, living essentially such a life as many thousands have lived here be-

The Multitude of Our Thoughts Hidden

fore you, and as many thousands are contemporaneously living—a life cast in the mold of the ordinary academic routine. There is nothing specially remarkable in it, you would say; nothing much for the imagination to expatiate upon; nothing to make a novel out of, still less a poem; yet, beyond question, if you knew the realities that in the fellowship of every day come close to you, nay, if you knew what is around you at this moment,—what thoughts, what experiences, representative of the deepest passion and pathos of human life,—you would be struck with a great amazement; you would stare at one another.

In attributing the hue and quality of impressive significance to our life I have thus far, with myself, been referring to those circumstances and events that lie out of view in the background of personal *history*. But there are other phases of life under the surface—universal, omnipresent, at any rate with such as we—that when pondered must magnify our conception of its contents. The

The Gospel's View of Our Life

thoughts, for instance, *upon* life that all of us day by day are thinking—what thoughts they are and how do they follow us! Take the thought of our *mortality*, and what a place it holds in every mind that has the faculty of reflection! I suppose there is not one of us who does not ordinarily many times between each waking and sleeping distinctly recognize and in some fashion survey his situation as the heir of an earthly existence that is transient and passing. Morning, noon, and night we look that fact in the face. It is an element of our self-consciousness, the thought of it. It walks the street with us; it goes into company with us; it comes between us and the page we are reading; it mingles with our work and with our play. The man you meet and talk or joke with has in all probability within the hour been visited by it, as you have been, and as you both will be again within the hour ensuing. It may stay with you an instant only, but, wherever you are and however you are engaged from one year's end to the other, there occurs no long

The Thought of Mortality

interval in which it does not step from behind its curtain and exchange glances with you. And life so punctuated with the sense of mortality is something more than humdrum.

Again, those whom we pass and repass in the to and fro of our and their common days have their thoughts, and many thoughts, as do we, on the things of this strange world and of human experience that it is not possible to see through, that are enigmatic, unfathomable. Certainly they do; why not? And people in all walks, of all conditions. In one of the actor Edwin Booth's letters, published not long since, he says: "Life is a great big spelling-book, and on every page we turn the words grow harder to understand the meaning of." He adds, speaking from a religious faith which I believe he had: "But there *is* a meaning, and when the last leaf flops over we'll know the whole lesson." That feeling of his, so vividly expressed, with which, notwithstanding the distractions of his calling, he communed, which no doubt went on and came off the stage with him sometimes, and which grew deeper as he grew older—you all understand it perfectly. And it is everywhere; it is an ingredient of human life as we know it.

But ah, if the *moral* facts, the moral experiences, that exist and are realities present in the persons of those whose lives are mingled in any community, in this community of yours, were uncovered, what aspects of life, to clothe it with another character than it wears to superficial view, would, we must suppose, then appear! We cannot, indeed, tell what, save in one instance, i.e., ourselves. But we can conjecture; we have the means of conjecturing. It is in the moral province that men, that associates, have least knowledge of one another individually. These all alike live hiddenly to a very great extent, and necessarily so. I do not now mean a purposed concealment, but that which is natural. But behind the mask, the veil of that privacy is what, were it seen, would make it impossible for us ever to look on life as a commonplace affair. In those to whom

The Invisible Facts around Us

we speak our "Good morning" and "How are you" as they go by us, or with whom we transact, we are all the while meeting things that are of evil and darkness—things also that are of goodness and light.

We meet sin, desires of sin, choices of sin, consciences in the torment of self-accusation, consciences growing seared by wicked works. We meet falsehood, ugly resentment, black envy, cruel malice, degrading sensuality. We meet haunting, wretched secrets and the miserable fears that wait upon them.

We meet other secrets too, and immeasurably different ones: happy secrets; secrets of the desire and choice of truth, integrity, and all righteousness; rejections of sin, repentances, sweet approvals of conscience, purposes of duty, girdings of the spirit for the battle with temptation; unfathomable pure and tender affections; charities, generosities, forgivenesses—the higher nature prevailing over the lower.

What is met in us, I repeat, we know, and God knows; but all these so opposite things

The Gospel's View of Our Life

we do daily and hourly meet in the familiar paths of the fellowship of life. We do not see them any more than we see those other contents of life that lie under the surface, of which I have spoken, but they are there. And they are what makes our common humanity a great matter—truly a matter no less than tragic. I do not say that we ought to see them, or that we can. As I have remarked, we could hardly live, or live together, if we did. But what I would say is that it is in their light that God sees our life and that the gospel of Christ sees it. It was one of Christ's divine marks that "he needed not that any one should bear witness concerning man, for he knew what was in man," and the word of his gospel is addressed to our secret thoughts, our secret hearts. That is the reason of the emotion that fills it. That is why it is so infinitely serious in its strain. It speaks ever from the standpoint of its view of our inward man. It brings us its sympathies, it brings us its offers of help, accordingly.

Speaks to the Inward Man

If any have troubles, deep, distressful, that they do not tell, that they may not tell, but must bear alone, He whose voice this gospel is, is not ignorant of them. "O trembling, weary, burdened mortal," it whispers, "your pain and sorrow are not hid; there is a rich and tender divine compassion brooding over you, following you every step of your way. Ever at your side, though unseen, is your heavenly Father and Redeemer. Cast your care on him, for he careth for you."

If we have our dark questions, and are pressed by the weight of life's mystery, and oftentimes know not what to think of it all, the gospel understands that burden too, and appreciates it wholly, and feels deeply for us under its oppression, and has a great deal to say—more than any other teacher—to lighten the load of it.

If we have sins, sins of heart and of life, that are unguessed by our fellow-men, that are our guilty secret, to the eye the gospel turns upon us they are naked and open every one. It knows all about them, and all our

The Gospel's View of Our Life

unhappy and fearful thoughts arising from them. And in them likewise it feels for us intensely, and regarding them it has much to say, most plainly, most earnestly, and in perfect kindness, if we will listen to it, that is just what we need to hear.

And if, in the midst of our earthly pursuits, participations, and hopes we are in our deep heart honestly wishing and striving after goodness, and, though by reason of our frailty failing oft, are holding on that way, cherishing the aim and resolve of a better obedience to all duty, the gospel penetrates that secret; and there is not a thought we have, not a difficulty we contend with, not a doubt or fainting we fall into, that it does not comprehend completely, for which it has not instant encouragement and aid, as some of you, I am persuaded, have found out.

In short, in its reckoning our life is, far above all else, the life so manifold, so checkered, so full of lights and shadows, that is lived within. There is the main flow and volume of it. To us as in that life, so much

A Gospel for Every Soul

of which is unknown, and must be, except to ourselves and to God, yet that comprehends the bulk of our total experience and all its heights and depths,—that life which, as our souls are acquainted with it, has such room for the message of eternal grace, mercy, and peace,—it draws near and speaks. It appeals to us in the name of our supreme and most intimate personal realities, if we do but consider. And so is it not a gift most practical and most precious—a gospel for us and for humanity?

Trophies of Youth the Safeguard of Manhood

By

Rev. James G. K. McClure,
Pastor of the Lake Forest (Ill.) Presbyterian Church

"And the priest said, The sword of Goliath the Philistine, whom thou slewest in the valley of Elah, behold, it is here wrapped in a cloth behind the ephod: if thou wilt take that, take it: for there is no other save that here. And David said, There is none like that; give it me."—1 Sam. xxi. 9.

IN her gymnasium Yale has a trophy-room. Many a graduate feels his blood stirred as he enters it. The emblems of contest, flag and cup, oar and ball, arouse the memory. Scenes of the past become vivid—the surging crowd, the excited faces, the shouts of victory. Other days are lived over again, and there is joy and inspiration in recalling them.

The setting up of trophies is a custom as

James G. K. McClure

The Hour of Contest

old as history; all ancient peoples did it. The Greeks put shields and helmets on a tree of the battle-ground if it was a land victory, and beaks of conquered vessels on the nearest coast if it was a sea victory. The Romans did differently. They carried their trophies to some prominent spot in Rome itself. Still differently did the Egyptians and the Israelites, who deposited their trophies in their temples.

So it was that the sword taken by youthful David from conquered Goliath was in the tabernacle. What stirring scenes that sword suggested! A young man going out alone to meet a vaunting foe. Two armies, Philistines and Israelites, numbering thousands, on opposite hills, watching the unevenly matched contestants. The slinging of a smooth stone, its sinking into Goliath's forehead, the giant's fall, David's springing forward to draw Goliath's sword. Surely that was a moment never to be forgotten when, with the giant's head in his left hand, David held aloft the giant's sword in his right hand, and there

Trophies of Youth

burst from the throats of Israel the shout of victory that sent dismay to the hearts of the Philistines and made them as leaves before the hurricane to the onrushing Israelites.

Henceforth that sword of Goliath was a trophy. It stood for victory. The people placed it in their most sacred building, that the sight of it might call to mind a past triumph and arouse to new courage. There it was, behind the sacred robe of divination, well wrapped in protecting cloths.

Years passed, and David, no more a ruddy youth, but now a care-marked man, seeks refuge in this very tabernacle where is Goliath's sword. Reverses have come to him. Instead of being a favorite he is an exile fleeing before envy and hate for his life. He has not one weapon of defense. He begs the priest in charge to give him some piece of armor. The priest answers that but one weapon is in his keeping—the sword of Goliath. David's heart bounds at the mention of that trophy. "There is none like that; give it me," he says. As his hand touches it he

The Joy of Victory

becomes a new man. His courage reasserts itself. Cheered by the memory of what he once had done with it, he now bravely faces his difficulties. The trophy of his youth has become the inspiration of his manhood.

Youth-time trophies! It is Southey who says: " Live as long as you may, the first twenty years form the greater part of your life. They appear so when they are passing; they seem to have been so when we look back to them; and they take up more room in our memory than all the years which succeed them." Victories won then mean more than victories won later. Never is a man so conscious of the sweets of triumph and so elated by the joys of success as in his earlier years. The shout that greeted David when he conquered Goliath sank deeper into his heart and memory than any shout he ever heard afterward. To succeed in the contests of youth, whatever their sphere, social, literary, political, athletic, is to have an experience of pleasure that is scarcely surpassed in all one's life.

Trophies of Youth

Besides, youth is like the Nile's springtime, when the fullness of the river gives opportunity to store away for the coming drought. In youth virtues and experiences can be laid up for the crises of life. Only as hope and courage are accumulated then are they in reserved force for sudden difficulty and trial. The soldier who in camp does not learn to handle his rifle will be helpless in the confusion of battle. Insurance cannot be obtained when flames are bursting out of the house. He who does not strive for victories in youth stands small show of victories in manhood. For time is a current bearing the yesterdays into to-days and the to-days into to-morrows. The present is the future, carrying it in itself as the seed carries the flower. A to-morrow unconnected with to-day is unthinkable. The flower that is to be must have somewhere a seed that now is. Youth is the seed of manhood, and what we lay up, or fail to lay up, in youth determines what we shall have, or shall fail to have, in manhood.

What, then, are these trophies to be won

A Sound Body

in youth for manhood's safeguard? Physical strength is one. Without it no mature man can do his best work. Youth, with its warm blood, vigorous vitality, strong appetite, restful sleep, may be a very magazine of power. The wear and tear of physical strain have not come yet. While they tarry a young man may fortify himself for them by accumulations of health which later will be a storehouse of resource.

Such being the case, it is no slight matter to hurt one's physical vigor either by neglect or abuse. Many men have broken down within five years of leaving college, and become impaired, if not useless, because they did not treasure their health while here. Scores have fallen by the wayside later because of the recklessness with which they spent their buoyant energy. Sickness and death are indeed inevitable to every one, but there is no necessity for soliciting their approach. Death walks as near the young man's back as the old man's face, but why urge him to overtake us? That law of God that makes physical decay the penalty of physical wrong is unbreakable. Dissipation of vital energy inevitably ends in physical deterioration. A young man cannot let any bodily passion run away with him and expect to be safe, any more than a child letting a spirited horse take the bit in his teeth to run as he will can expect to escape peril. A man's body is God's temple, and God never allows sacrilege to his temple to go unchallenged and uncondemned. But if with earnest desire to conserve its sacredness a man stores away all possible physical vigor, he will find in after-years, as David found with Goliath's sword, that the purity and self-control of his youth stand him in good stead in the hours of exposure.

Intellectual discipline is another trophy to be won in youth. Let the distinction between discipline and knowledge be kept clear. What an educated youth needs is capability to apply his mind—investigating, comparing, combining, drawing deductions—and then to put the full force of that mind into the work

Ability to Think

undertaken. Better than universal knowledge is power to use limited knowledge. Too much knowledge there cannot be, but knowledge without the ability to use it is an impediment, not a help. He who fails in youth to learn how to ponder facts and arrange them is at a great disadvantage when caught in the hurry and competition of after-years. Neither merchants nor engineers, generals nor scholars, can do their work successfully with minds undisciplined. As much solid, penetrating thought may be required in railroading as in teaching, in banking as in editing. The success of a college youth in the industry to which he gives himself will depend largely on his power to think. If he acquires that, then he may go whithersoever Providence calls him and he need not be afraid to attempt his work. The man who can use aright two facts will always be stronger than the man who has a hundred facts, but who cannot use them.

And now for moral trophies. One such is habits. In youth we form them, and then in age they form us. At first they are our method of life, and at last they are our life itself. Once they involved conscious effort, later they seem automatic. Care entered into the first writing of our signature, but now we write that signature almost as unconcernedly as a machine prints.

Habits of good can thus become the protection of our maturity. They are the chief dependence on which a man must rely for his own right conduct when circumstances call for such speedy action that he cannot stop to analyze the motives that guide him. If temptation to do evil suddenly assails one habituated to the good, the chances are that he will continue on in the habit of the good. For there are hundreds of good things which the human heart may do so regularly and persistently that they become a very part of the heart, shaping its opinions, controlling its desires, and deciding its affections.

One such special habit is that of reverence. Reverence is treating worthy things worthily, and the most worthy things the most worthily.

The Mission of Reverence

The command "not to take the name of the Lord in vain" teaches that God, the best, should be treated as the best. It is an injunction to have good judgment, to estimate persons and things aright, and to act toward the noblest and greatest as though they were the noblest and greatest. Such a habit of discriminating thought and conduct, once acquired, is a ceaseless blessing. It secures a just valuation of all objects to be considered, and it prevents men from looking upon ten as though it were fifty, on the mole-hill as though it were a mountain, on the transient as though it were permanent, on evil as though it were good.

Happy the man who early acquires reverence for purity. To consider spotlessness as insignificant is to have the whole judgment demoralized. Impure thought, once become a fixed element of life, will color all vision and lower all ideals, will make untrustworthy all our opinions of society and of individuals. But reverence for purity, once become a habit, will so permeate our nature that the low and lewd will have no hold upon our thought, and we shall wonder that any person can spoil his jokes with them or, still worse, soil his own mind with them.

Happy, too, the man who early acquires reverence for himself. When a young man adopts the habit of regarding every one of his appetites as a divine gift, bestowed for holy purposes, and will not allow them to be diverted to wrong uses, it is an absolute impossibility that he ever become a drunkard or any kind of a profligate. Whatever is hurtful to himself will be esteemed base by him simply because it is hurtful. He will acquire a self-mastery that will give him a victor's sense of power. He will be too high-souled to mind low and dishonorable things. They may throng about him, but they cannot appeal to him.

This matter of reverence, what a safeguard it is when it is reverence for God and for what manifests God! Certainly no one may expect youth to estimate all objects as manhood does. Youth is not asked to be as sedate as age. Its very nature is sprightly. But if youth, whatever its sprightliness, will continually hold itself to a reverential use of God's name, of God's house, of God's worship, of God's Bible, yes, and of every fact that in nature, in the soul, and in history reveals God, youth will have laid up a condition of mind that will be its salvation when doubt contemptuously asks, "What is truth?" For if there is reverence for the real and an earnest purpose to exalt highest the best things of life, youth has a panoply that all the hosts of mental and moral confusion cannot pierce. But if there is no such reverence failure is sure. Once I saw my own classmate, urged to a stronger, better life, throw himself on a sofa and with tears in his eyes hopelessly answer: "It is no use. I cannot do it. I have yielded to wrong so often that I have no will power left. I cannot resolve to do right." It was a pitiful scene: a charming, popular young man looking for an instant beneath the surface of things, and helplessly declaring himself the slave of a powerless will! And all because throughout his youth he had habitually yielded to the poorer elements of his nature and had allowed an impotent will to become his *lasting* characteristic.

But there is one more sphere for youth-time trophies, and that a great one—memories. All youth is filling itself up with memories, but no youth seems to have such happy opportunities for memories as college youth. Memories! They are almost the largest, if not, in fact, the very largest, part of what a man keeps with him when long years have passed since he was a college youth. Why should those memories ever shame our hearts or injure our power in manhood? What a mistake that youth made who for fifteen minutes, out of mere curiosity, read a debasing book, and then afterward was obliged to say, " That book has haunted me like an evil specter ever since. I have asked God on my knees to obliterate that book from my mind, but I believe that I shall carry down the damage of those fifteen minutes to my grave"!

Good Memories a Defense

Good memories are strength and comfort. Moses, still untried, heard God speak a message of recognition and duty to him from a burning bush. Later, grown to be an old man and burdened with anxieties, Moses recalled that experience at the bush and it revived his faith and cheered his heart. It is in early years that God loves to put his voices into the soul, assuring us of his nearness, calling to us to be earnest, and arousing us to endeavors for our fellows. In more mature years we may be almost dazed by our disappointments, by the complexity and strife of business, by the unkindness and even falseness of our supposed friends. Then the temptation comes to us to question the goodness of God, to question the reality of the soul and the worth of self-denying effort. In such an hour what a help it is to look back and say, "Once I was in college, and there God came very close to me with his blessings. I felt him in my heart. And though I knew less of the world than now, still I had a tender conscience then; I was not embittered by life's rough usage; my motives were simple and pure"! That very memory steadies the soul like an anchorage. There are many men gone out from this college who to-day are helped to be noble by the recollection of what God enabled them to think and feel and do when they were students here, walking beneath these elms and entering these halls. God gave them glimpses of himself and of duty that make it impossible for them to doubt the reality of God and the joy of his service.

A white-haired Yale man loved to tell this story. In his undergraduate days he led a classmate to the new life of a Christian. That classmate became a wise and influential leader. He blessed society and the church by his Christian earnestness. He, in turn, led many others to the Christian life. What a trophy was this of ever-accumulating power laid up in youth for the world's good! "Bury my influence with me," said a man once vicious, but now repentant. He was dying, but his influence could not be buried with him. It

Christian Character a Trophy

was a living thing that would not die. John Newton corrupted a companion when on board the ship *Harriet*. Later, when John Newton had reformed, he met the one he had corrupted and tried to undo the evil he had done, but he failed.

Noble Christian character! Who will lay up this trophy now? It *is* a trophy, never coming of itself, but won, and won through contest. There are five inclinations, Horace says, that must be fought in this contest. His words are: "Youth yields to every evil impression, is rough to reproof, is slow in attending to his best interests, is presumptuous, and is swift to leave what before has pleased his fancy." These are the inclinations to be conquered. They are conquered when youth (1) resists evil, (2) values reproof, (3) hastens to do right, (4) seeks divine guidance, and (5) cleaves to the good. The very impetuosity and passion of youth, turned from wrong uses into right uses, help us to win our trophies.

Win them, then, as David won Goliath's

sword. Go forth to life in the name and under the inspiration of God. Have open eyes to see the evils that threaten God's kingdom in the world. Face those evils. You know full well that God wishes their overthrow. Do not hesitate to enter the field against them. Advance upon them before the fascination of fear paralyzes you. Thousands may stand irresolute, but do you dare and do. If none else act, go forward alone. Use the skill you have, simple though it seem, and do your best. What if no voice does speak to you from the skies, indicating duty? It is enough that there is an evil needing overthrow. Meet it with the soul of a knight. God's eye is on you; God's heart is with you. To conquer is to give cheer to all God's Israel. To-day and now do the deeds and win the experiences that to-morrow will be your joy and salvation.

Manhood's Struggle and Victory

By

S. E. Herrick, D.D.
Pastor of the Mount Vernon Church, Boston, Mass.

The Lamb made war with the beast.—Revelation, passim.

MY text, you observe, is not quoted, but extracted. It is a condensation in few words of extended passages of this remarkable book. I have long felt that but little confidence is to be placed in any minute and particularizing interpretation of its picturesque and amazing scenery. The book has been the favorite exercise-ground for the ingenuity and wilfulness of exegetical cranks and prediction-mongers through all the centuries. It has been the arsenal, moreover, whence sectarian virulence and theological hatred have drawn their weapons of nickname and threat and invective. The beast, the dragon, the scarlet woman, Babylon the Great—these names have been affixed in the history of theological or ecclesiastical warfare to this party and to that, sometimes, no doubt, in the spirit of sincere and thoughtful interpretation, but quite as often under the inspiration of that animosity which so often attends religious differences among people nominally Christian. Romanists and Protestants alike have picked up stones out of this field to throw at each other. Lope de Vega, a most devoted Catholic, celebrated the privateering exploits of the Protestant Sir Francis Drake in an epic poem which he called "The Dragontea," punning upon Sir Francis's name, in which he is made to fill the part of the great red dragon of the Apocalypse, and is threatened with that monster's fate as the enemy of God and man. In the same poem Queen Elizabeth figures as the "scarlet lady of Babylon."

But various and contradictory as have been the interpretations of most of the great figures which throng the gorgeous canvas of

The Lamb and the Beast

the revelator, there is one, the chief figure, which appears more than a score of times, concerning which, through all the ages, there has been no difference of opinion. That is *the Lamb*. Assuming that the great vision, or series of visions, was seen and described by John, the author of the fourth gospel, there can be no doubt as to the meaning with which this great central figure was charged in his mind. The Lamb is manifestly the eternal Christ—the infinite gentleness and patience and long-suffering, and spirit of sacrifice, which is central and intimate in Godhood, which was once, visibly to mortals, condensed and expressed in the historic life of Jesus of Nazareth—" the Lamb of God," i.e., the Lamb which is in God's nature eternally, without beginning and without end. This gentle and yet august figure appears and reappears throughout the book, and often in positions of startling incongruity. He stands " a Lamb as it had been slain "—what so helpless?—and yet in the midst of the throne, in the place of supreme eminence, from the foundation of the world. It is the Lamb, again, that opens the seven-sealed book of heaven's mysteries. It is the Lamb who stands as Bridegroom—his wife the new Jerusalem, ever descending out of heaven from God. It is the Lamb that is the lamp and glory of the celestial city, in the midst of whose light the nations are to walk. It is the Lamb—type of all gentleness—from whose wrath kings and princes and tribunes hide themselves and entreat rocks and mountains to shelter them. And finally, it is the Lamb which again and again makes war with the beast, coming up now out of the earth and now out of the sea, and which finally overcomes and makes him powerless for ever and ever.

The panorama is mystic, marvelous, amazing. I deem it a mistaken endeavor to attempt any refinement of interpretation. There is danger in dealing with such a picture too microscopically. Symbolism too often runs into wilfulness. The tremors of

The Lamb and the Beast

the pencil are sometimes magnified into essentials, while really grand essentials are lost sight of. In the portrayal of a regenerating world what matters it whether or no we can discover all at once the special significance of the jacinth, the amethyst, and the beryl, the seven heads and ten horns of the beast, the seven vials and the falling stars, and the twelve manner of fruits that are growing upon the tree of life? What we want is to let the grand sweep and spiritual movement of the picture into our thought and life. While the glories of a magnificent park like the Yosemite or the Yellowstone are around one, it is not best to devote much time to the microscopic investigation of a single flower or the striæ of a beetle's wing-case. It seems to me that we have here the cartoon of a master who does not care at present to reveal the significance of detail, but who wishes to convey his ideal of a great time-movement. He entitles his canvas at the outset "The Revelation of Jesus Christ." And the core of that revelation is "the

Manhood's Struggle and Victory

Lamb making war with the beast." This warfare and its issues constitute the underlying unity of the whole book.

And the beast? Well, the beast is the *beast;* the beast which is the basal element in human life, which made human life possible, and the struggle with which and the conquest of which make an angelic life possible. The conquest of the beast by the Lamb is the meaning of all history in its larger aspect and of all individual biography. The interest which attaches to every piece of biographical literature arises from the fact that it shows how the battle went in some particular case. This Book of Revelation is for this reason in some grand sense a summary of all human history, as it is also a typical picture of all personal struggle. In fact, no novel, no romance, was ever written that proved of any interest, save as it made this conflict the burning problem of the story. It is the solution of this problem which chains your interest and makes you eager for the development of the plot and its

The Lamb and the Beast

culmination. When that is reached, and you have learned how the battle went, the author has nothing more that you care to read. A story that were purely human, or even purely angelic, would be too tame for earthly readers. We want to see the beast vanquished or transformed. We want to see the earthly, the sensual, the devilish, trampled down or regenerated. No stage-play was ever successful for long, no drama could ever get a place in literature, that did not awaken an interest in this age-long, world-wide, universal, and yet intensely personal contest between the Lamb and the beast. It is the truth which science emphasizes in its latest word about the struggle for existence and the survival of the fittest. History and science both have to do simply with this —the elimination of the beast and the enfranchisement of the Lamb. It is a terrific warfare, but only pessimism says that its issue is doubtful. "The meek shall inherit the earth." "The persecuted for righteousness' sake shall possess the kingdom of God."

Manhood's Struggle and Victory

If we take a large general retrospect of human history, its dominant and most impressive suggestion is the power of the beast, the beast *in* man, and the beast *over* man. And the beast is so exultant, so vigorous, and the man is so feeble and so vincible. The beast seems to be the steering power. Go through the roods of Oriental sculpture, say in the British Museum, in which ancient civilizations have left the enduring records of their life and their religion. Everywhere man and beast are joined indissolubly, and the beast is evidently the groom and governor of the union—bulls with human heads, the faces of men joined with the swift wing and ferocious talons of ravenous and unclean birds, sphinxes in which humanity seems to be trying to paw itself free from its bestiality, and yet to be helplessly held back by the superior force of the brutishness. And the fauns and satyrs and tritons and centaurs of classic fable are reminiscences of the same great fact in man's spiritual history. The great empire upon whose ruins, and largely

The Lamb and the Beast

out of whose materials, our modern civilization has been constructed, with great pride and in good faith traced its origin to the infants that were suckled by the wolf. And nine tenths of the scutcheons of the Old World to-day still perpetuate the story of this old consciousness of the power of the beast, and instead of their shame, as it is, treat it as their glory, with their dragons and their griffins and their lions and their vultures and their bulls and wild boars. We pass these things by as the unmeaning relics of a dead mythology. But they are not mythical or dead or unmeaning. They are in every case the assertion of the power of the beast in the history of man's nature, religion, and life. They constitute the pictorial history of human animalism. They are a part of the same heraldic blazonry which fills this Book of the Revelation.

And the facts are not dead which they represent. Beasthood may vary its prevalent form from time to time, but it exists in some form. Look around us. It is beasthood—

Manhood's Struggle and Victory

how it shall be controlled and kept under, how it shall be transformed or cast out—that constitutes the problem of government and of society in all our large communities. The trail of the dragon winds through all our streets, and his poisonous breath meets one at every turn. We can hardly keep it from our purest and most secluded homes, and over what numberless habitations it broods as a constant atmosphere, poisoning all domesticity, making households bitter and hearts hopeless.

And it is not simply a social and governmental problem, which you and I can hold off and look upon from afar with more or less complacency. It is the one problem of all personal life. Some of us can look into faces made dear by years of pleasant companionship or by ties of birth and blood, and watch with solicitude the fortunes of this strange warfare with the beast. No joy of life so high and solemn as that with which we discern the tokens of his weakening. No woe so grave, so intolerable, as that which crushes our

The Lamb and the Beast

hearts within us as we see manhood or womanhood going down under the impulses of animalism—becoming "earthly, sensual, and devilish." Nay, we all know this power in ourselves. We are conscious of the beast in us. We have experienced the tigerish rage, the swinish selfishness, the unfeeling hardness, the retaliating impulses, the low passions, mounting up and over our better and purer thoughts and threatening the extinction of the divine. We all know it. The best men in the world have felt the conflict most deeply. St. Paul did fight with beasts at Ephesus, and everywhere else. St. George did slay the dragon, and more than one or two. St. Anthony did feel the thrust of the swinish snouts and the tearing of tigers' and vultures' claws, which Albert Durer painted in his terrible but true picture of the saint's temptation. It is the story of Hercules and his labors, and of the Son of man in his forty days' temptation in the wilderness.

Now it is against the beast that the eternal Lamb makes his war, and will until he is conquered and cast out forever. A strange conception that, and one that almost shocks us by its incongruity—a lamb warring against a beast, with the purpose and expectation of overcoming him. It requires a good deal of effort to adjust our thoughts to it. And yet it is but saying in another and bolder way that God loves a bad world into goodness; that he does not, after all, depend upon the machinery of legislation and penalty and police to drive men out of their sins and sensualisms. Force is not remedy. Shutting a soul up under such mere mechanical conditions that it would be impossible for it to do sinful things would be but a sort of half-way victory. Shutting up the Jack-in-the-box does not in any real sense change Jack; the hideous and repulsive thing is still there just under the lid. The warfare of the Lamb with the beast must be such war as a lamb can make. The force by which the contest is to be carried on and the victory gained is not dynamic, but moral, affectional. The life is not to be crushed in compulsions, as one

The Lamb and the Beast

might break up the ice of a river, but it is to be melted in the sunshine of love and grace and patience. Hence such expressions as " having a heart washed in the blood of the Lamb " have their real significance—a significance which has been often obliterated by mechanical interpretations. The only way in which a lamb can fight a beast is to patiently shed his blood in meek endurance. Christ fights sin and conquers sin by his cross and passion. The figure finds its true interpretation in the story of the prodigal son. The beast in him was only conquered when his father—patient, long-suffering, anguish-stricken at his heart—fell upon the boy's neck and kissed him and wept over him. It was the heart's blood of the father that washed away the sin of the son.

> "The patience of immortal love
> Outwearies mortal sin."

And men are slowly learning this great fact, that the war with the beast is to be the *Lamb's* war. This is the temper of all the earnest efforts which are now making in civil-

Manhood's Struggle and Victory

ized communities toward social reform and betterment. Men are learning that heart's blood must be shed in the battle. Compassionate love goes further than great strenuousness. They are learning that no throne or seat of authority and compulsion and force can accomplish much that has not a bleeding lamb in the center of it. *War* as *war* fails. War as co-passion disarms and subdues even the beast. You recall Whittier's version of the Indian story:

> " Once, on the errands of his mercy bent,
> Buddha, the holy and benevolent,
> Met a fell monster, huge and fierce of look,
> Whose awful voice the hills and forests shook.
> ' O son of peace!' the giant cried, ' thy fate
> Is sealed at last, and love shall yield to hate.'
> The unarmed Buddha, looking, with no trace
> Of fear or anger, in the monster's face,
> In pity said, ' *Poor fiend, even thee I love.*'
> Lo! as he spake the sky-tall terror sank
> To handbreadth size; the huge abhorrence shrank
> Into the form and fashion of a dove;
> And where the thunder of its rage was heard,
> Circling above him sweetly sang the bird.
> ' Hate hath no harm for love,' so ran the song;
> ' And peace unweaponed conquers every wrong!' "

And yet this pitying love is no weak thing. Brightest light is backed by darkest shadow.

The Lamb and the Beast

Tenderest pity goes hand in hand with most strenuous and uncompromising hate. The more intense the love for any object, the more consuming the wrath against whatever assails the well-being of that object. There is no wrath like the "wrath of the Lamb." It must needs be mighty. It is the shield which infinite love interposes for the protection of the human spirit from its worst enemy. It is the blast which saves the wheat and drives away the chaff. It is the fire which spares every atom of the gold and burns out its dross and defilement. There is no friendlier word of Holy Writ than that "our God is a consuming fire."

Now this, whether you find it in India or in Judea, is *the gospel of Jesus Christ.* It is *the Lamb of God who taketh away the sins of the world.* It is of no lasting use to fight the beast with the beast, in the world, in those who are specially near and dear to us, or in ourselves. As for the beast that is abroad in the world, he is still rampant, terrible; but there are signs everywhere that the Lamb is

Manhood's Struggle and Victory

on the field, and his patient work grows, like a dawn upon the darkness. As for the beast in those around us, there must be no heat of anger, no resentment of the beastliness. Cudgeling will only make a cur more currish. We must carry toward them a bleeding lamb in our hearts. As for the beast in ourselves, "If we walk in the Spirit," says the apostle, "we shall not fulfil the lusts of the flesh." And "walking in the Spirit" is nothing more or less than letting the gentleness, the purity, the tenderness, and grace of God's slain Lamb enter in and possess and dominion our souls. He asks each one of us, as he asked one of old, "Wilt thou?" And to the assent heartily given he responds, "I will; be thou clean."

The Sabbath

By

Bishop John H. Vincent
Topeka, Kan.

"And he said unto them, The Sabbath was made for man, and not man for the Sabbath: so that the Son of man is lord even of the Sabbath."—Mark ii. 27, 28.

JESUS himself kept, in his own way, the Sabbath of the Jews. It was his custom on that day to attend the services of the synagogue. In the lesson of the day we have a hint as to his habit from boyhood in the town "where he had been brought up." In the record from which the text is taken we find him and his disciples walking through the fields on the Sabbath day, plucking the bending wheat-heads as they passed. Jesus more than once gave offense to his fellow-countrymen by his independence of ceremo-

The Sabbath

nial requirements. He wrought works of mercy and of necessity on Sabbath days which if not specifically forbidden were to a faithful Pharisee of doubtful propriety. His enemies tried to entrap him, that they might condemn him; but he claimed that good deeds were proper on a good day; that the Sabbath was made for man, and not man for the Sabbath; and that he, the Son of man, was lord of the Sabbath. The followers of Christ, released from the bondage of Jewish enactments and customs, used the Sabbath for special Christian services, and later on observed the first day of the week, which gradually became the Christian way of fulfilling the Sabbatical obligation. We find the recognition of the Sabbath in the earliest records of the Jewish (which is also in its essential elements the Christian) faith. In the very beginning, when the first notation of time was made, and man began to live and to order affairs on the planet, the Sabbath was instituted. It began with the race. In the immortal song of creation found on the first page of the

The Day of Genesis

Book of Genesis two facts are made clear: first, that God was the Creator, and second, that the creation was a gradual, a progressive movement. To aid human thought and to make impressive the idea of gradualness, the sacred writer introduces a time-scale. This "day" of the first chapter of Genesis has nothing to do with an actual "period," whether of twenty-four hours or twenty-four millions of years. It is a beautiful device—this use of a week of days and nights—to show that the creation was not instantaneous. The writer might have introduced any other time-measurement. He might have suggested years, or centuries, or cycles. But the most convenient, the simplest scale was the week of days—a figure to help us to the thought of continuous creative energy.

On the "sixth day" man appears. He is a higher creation. He is made in the image of God. He is to be on earth the representative of God in dominion—one with God; having knowledge, in his measure, like God's knowledge, life like God's life, authority like

The Sabbath

God's authority, and the possibility of righteousness like God's righteousness. And how shall man be helped to a true conception of a godlike life—a life, not of indolence, but of strength, repose, and peace? How shall man, with this wealth of material resources, be reminded of his spiritual endowment, mission, and dependence? How shall he be brought into a life of communion with God, his Maker, his Father—a life above the physical life; a life for the development of his spiritual nature, derived from God; a life nobler than a life of physical, commercial, social, political interest and activity; a life of preparation for all other and lower relations and responsibilities? And if man made innocent shall, when tested, fail of virtue and drop to lower levels, how shall he be brought up to righteousness and true holiness? Therefore the inspired poet of the creation added to his time-scale another day—a seventh day, a Lord's day, a day of divine rest and of human opportunity. It was not a day of God's withdrawal from his

Paul and the Sabbath

universe, a day of the suspension of divine interest and activity. It was an impressive symbol of human need and of the true rest of the soul of man—godlike only when in perfect harmony and communion with him. Thus the primeval Sabbath was instituted as a reminder of man's high relationships, and as a help to his highest training for dominion on the earth and for the unutterable glories of his destiny beyond. How insignificant do Sunday laws about "things" appear when we grasp the larger thought of Genesis and of Jesus, that the Sabbath was made for man, and not man for the Sabbath! This same view Paul and the early Christians held. The study of that apostle's theory, as set forth in the fourteenth chapter of his letter to the Romans, will show his attitude toward the ritualistic Sabbath of the Pharisees, while we see clearly in his teachings and habits that he exalted the spiritual life of divine communion which the true Sabbath of the Scriptures is appointed to promote.

The same misapprehensions and contro-

The Sabbath

versies which caused discussions between Jesus and the Pharisees, and between Paul and the Judaizing Christians of his day, have continued in the church until the present day. And while such theories remain disputations, extremes and excesses are inevitable. Those who believe in the divine provision of the sacred seventh of our time for the higher uses of man cannot approve the indifference and opposition of men who would abolish all recognition of the Sabbath day. Men who carry their ethical and religious convictions into political and civic life, who make it a matter of conscience to seek the enactment of good laws, and the execution of them when enacted, are sure to array against themselves and their measures men who carry the idea of liberty beyond the limits of social security. And these same good and true representatives of the higher social and personal life are in danger of insisting too strenuously upon religious regulations which contravene both religious and political liberty. So it happens that severity remonstrates against

Laxity in Sabbath Observance

laxity and sometimes enacts and enforces restrictive laws, and men who are not religious, or at least not religious after the religious ways of their neighbors, feel that their personal freedom is interfered with. Citizens of foreign birth, accustomed to the more easygoing social ways and the less rigid religious notions of their native lands beyond the sea, protest freely against what they call an infringement of their rights in a free republic—less free, they aver, in these respects than the monarchical governments they left in order to become citizens of this great nation of freemen.

This foreign element, but not this alone, will account for the increasing laxity of our age touching Sabbath observance. We are all aware of a reaction from the old-time strictness in the ordering of domestic life, and especially on the holy day. And this reaction is not wholly evil. We have pictures, not always exaggerated, of the early times: of the silent house on the Sabbath; the cold and frugal meal; the long hours

The Sabbath

spent in straight-backed pews in square-walled, square-windowed churches; long prayers, long sermons, long faces; sharp rebukes for smiles that could not be repressed, and solemn tones on Sundays from voices that on week-days were natural and agreeable. And all this—with sundry other public offices and private admonitions—conspired to make children loathe Sabbath days, sanctuary services, and home solemnities. People who had no such experiences themselves have heard and read about them and ridiculed them, and have reached the conclusion that Sabbath-keeping is a bondage and a folly—a bondage they purpose never to endure, a folly of which they will never be guilty. Thus what we call "society" laughs at the church; and as society is in the church, the church of to-day laughs at the church of yesterday, and we are in some danger of losing through a laugh what is really a serious and important factor in our civilization, physical, social, political, educational, religious—the true Sabbath day, the American Sabbath

Patriotism and the Sabbath

as distinguished from the Jewish, the European, and the Puritan Sabbath, the Sabbath of which John Ellerton sings:

> "This is the day of light: let there be light to-day;
> O Dayspring, rise upon our night, and chase its gloom away!
>
> "This is the day of rest: our failing strength renew,
> On weary brain and troubled breast shed thou thy freshening dew.
>
> "This is the day of peace: thy peace our spirits fill,
> Bid thou the blasts of discord cease, the waves of strife be still.
>
> "This is the first of days: send forth thy quickening breath,
> And wake dead souls to love and praise, O Vanquisher of death!"

Let us still honor and cherish the day of God, the sacred seventh of our treasure—*time!* All good things may be abused—learning and liberty and love. A nation's flag may be trailed in the dust. A nation's honor and courage may be tossed into the arena and played with by ambitious politicians to the humiliation of patriots. But learning, liberty, love, the nation's flag, and the nation's honor and courage, are good things. As we would save our land, let us save our Sabbath.

It does not matter what we call this day

The Sabbath

—"Sabbath," "Sunday," or "Lord's day." It matters not which day of the seven we hallow—"First-day" or "Seventh-day." It matters not at all which hours we keep—from sunset to sunset, or from midnight to midnight. But let us save the "sacred seventh"! Are there not wise reasons for trying to do this? And is there not a wise way of doing it? It is greatly in our favor that we still have the Sabbath with us. It is an institution long cherished; maintained by wise and good men; recently revived in Paris by a society of advanced French reformers who, although not churchmen, nor committed to any form of religious worship, are convinced that the French working-man must have one day a week for physical rest and social life. The Sabbath is in the legislation of all Christian lands, and the more the Bible is studied, the more plainly appears the reasonableness, the righteousness, the necessity of a day made for man—for man made in the image of God.

Our own busy and exciting American life

Its Symbolic Significance

especially needs the calming power of such a day. The tension of the times demands relief. Worn-out bodies, overtaxed brains, constantly stimulated energies, require some social regulation to compel recuperative rest. How fully are these requirements met in Sabbath stillness, religious reflection, the subduing power of sacred music, the impressive solemnities of public worship, the joy of home life, the memories of a past now hallowed by a love that was faithful in its day to its opportunity and that now draws the soul toward heaven!

The Sabbath day is a symbol of the highest and holiest verities in which man can be concerned. It is a monument in time, rising like the white obelisk in Washington from the dust and clamor of the earth toward the serene and stainless realm above. It is a day that points upward to God and destiny. It reminds us of duty. It offers to us pardon for the past, peace in the present, and hope for an immortal future. It represents the righteousness that is indispensable to the

The Sabbath

perpetuity of the republic. It represents "heaven and earth in union: earth for heaven, heaven for earth." Let the flag of the nation float! Its intrinsic value is slight; its significance beyond expression. Let the day of days, God's Sabbath, stand! It is but a shred of time; it is weighted with treasures of eternity.

The Sabbath is the day of opportunity. Its recognition by the community confers immense privilege on the individual. It withdraws the pressure of worldly occupation and drudgery, and leaves the man free to go, if he will, into the house of God "with the multitude that keeps holyday." It brings people together in that holiest fellowship, the fraternity of worship: parents and children, friends and neighbors, classes of society which the cares of the world elsewhere separate into castes—merchant and clerk, employer and employee. Alas, alas! that I dream of the possible rather than of the actual. But this is the Sabbath ministry of good neighborship, of good Samaritanship,

Its Sacred Opportunities

which makes it the day of the Son of man. The Sabbath is opportunity for the reverent, the associated, the private study of the most important fields of thought to which man's attention is called. For this we have books, sermons, classes, and may enjoy friendly religious conversation and discussion. What possibilities crowd the hours of the Sabbath!

The day makes possible personal growth in faith and sympathy and unselfishness. Is there a thoughtful man who does not periodically retire from the confusion of life into secret chambers of reflection, of prayer, and of resolve? Sabbath hours give him time for this high service and furnish incentives to its performance. What a corrective such sacred endeavors are of all tendencies to irreverence, to frivolity, to flippancy, to heedlessness, in matters of religious faith! What personal dignity is promoted by this personal fellowship with the God who made him, the Christ who redeemed him, and the Holy Spirit who dwells within him! Thus the Sabbath opens to the devout soul treasures

The Sabbath

of grace—the spirit of earnestness, of faith, of resoluteness. The American Sabbath is preëminently the opportunity of the American home. May we too easily abandon the old-time systematic ordering of the Sunday life at home? May we become careless in this respect? Better the old-time rigidity! Better for the children, better for the parents, better for the nation.

It is a good habit, this Sunday habit. It is hard to acquire in the beginning, as is all discipline in self-control and self-direction. Children are quite likely to rebel against the régime that is best for them. They may succeed in evading or in slipping the yoke of authority and then rejoice in their freedom. But such liberty is likely to become bondage in the end. It *is* good for a man to bear the yoke in his youth, in the home, in the schoolroom, in the field, in the shop. The parent is likely to know better than the child what ministers to personal strength and well-being. Infinite wisdom and love express in law what is best for man. That the best is for the present distasteful and often grievous is not strange, but it is folly to argue that because distasteful or even grievous it should be remitted. It is *not* a bad thing to train a boy in the decencies and proprieties of table manners, however strong the protests of the animal within him. It is not a bad thing to repress the fury of his temper and his unreasoning insubordination. A firm grip, a tone of authority, a withdrawal of coveted and otherwise legitimate pleasure, a physical demonstration of the reign of law and righteousness—these are wholesome lessons for the young brute who has wrapped up within him a man's reason, a potential conscience, and the germs of sainthood. Let us have fear in these days, not of too much home government, but of a carelessness which may, before we are aware of it, develop lawlessness. Let us have a Sabbath law and a Sabbath life at home. One cannot excuse the traditional puritanic rigidity concerning Sabbath observance; but for the sake of the children, by all that is beautiful and sacred in home love, by all that is divine in parental authority, by all that is imperative in moral obligation, let us make the day of God a sacred, a delightful, a memorable day in the family circle.

I have little patience with the questions in casuistry usually started when one speaks of the holy day and its sacred uses: "What about writing letters and studying lessons on Sunday?" "What about a Sunday afternoon walk with the children or friends, dining out, starting on a journey, reading the Sunday papers, street-car travel, conversing on secular topics?" and other questions of this class. Let all such questions be settled by the individual. As Paul says, "Let every man be fully persuaded in his own mind." There are many large and radical questions, far-reaching questions, which the man must answer before he comes to these minor matters, these merely symptomatic conditions— questions too numerous and too radical to allow us to waste time on these. Let a man ask himself, "Am I living an earnest life?

Sabbath Questionings

Have I faith in eternal things? Am I really theist or agnostic? Do I know the thoughts and reasonings of foremost philosophers, scientists, and saints who have believed in God, in revelation, in destiny? Again, what are the ruling motives in my life? Am I aiming at service or at self-advancement? Am I laying foundations of character that will stand the pressure of temptation in the years of public, social, or commercial life that lie before me? Am I excusing myself from personal investigation of the claims of religion because I happen to know of some scholarly and scientific man who openly repudiates those claims? What do I really know about Jesus of Nazareth? Is all the acquaintance with him I can lay claim to based upon some slight teaching in Sunday-school or upon some references I have heard in the pulpit? Do I know his place in history? Do I know only what Strauss or Renan has written concerning him, or is there a world of rich and reverent and scholarly literature the reading of which might modify my views of that great

The Sabbath

figure in human history who is to-day more talked about and thought about and written about than ever before or than any character in all history? Is it not worth my while to read what ten of the strongest and most gifted scholars of this generation have written in honor of this marvel of all history?" But I have suggested only a tithe of the questions an earnest soul ought to ask, and which a truly earnest soul *will* ask, in reference to the most momentous topics relating to human life. Here is the Sabbath day, with its splendid opportunities for reflection, reading, listening, conversing, on all these themes. Answer these questions and you will not be puzzled about street-cars, Sunday papers, Sunday dinners, or any of the usual small talk about Sabbath observance. Be tremendously in earnest, and topics will take their proper places, and some themes will drop out of sight, and others which you have never considered at all will loom up like mighty mountains on your horizon.

Young men, honor the Sabbath and let it

A Day of Rest

serve your higher nature. It was made for man. Receive it as God's provision for men who would be like God—knowing, loving, creating, exercising "dominion." Use it as a day of rest from the activities and perplexities of the lower realm of life, that you may rejoice in the higher and thus exalt the lower. Plato says, " Out of pity for the wretched life of mortals the Deity arranged days of festal refreshment." George Washington, at the beginning of the War of the Revolution, issued an order from which I quote: " That the troops may have an opportunity of attending public worship, as well as to take some rest after the great fatigue they have gone through, the general in future excuses them from fatigue duty on Sundays, except at the shipyards or on special occasions, until further orders. We can have but little hope of the blessing of Heaven on our arms if we insult it by our impiety and folly." Well says Ralph Waldo Emerson, " Christianity has given us the Sabbath, the jubilee of the whole world, whose light dawns welcome alike into

The Sabbath

the closet of the philosopher, into the garret of toil, and into prison-cells, and everywhere suggests even to the vile the dignity of spiritual being." Robertson of Brighton, whose insight into spiritual philosophy was as direct and penetrating as his practical surrender to its teachings was complete, says of Sabbath observance: "I am more and more sure by practical experience that the reason for the observance of the Sabbath lies deep in the everlasting necessities of human nature, and that as long as man is man the blessedness of keeping it, not as a day of rest only, but as a day of spiritual rest, will never be annulled."

Therefore let us, sons of men, sons of God, keep with reverent care and with the joy of love this holy day—this Sabbath that was made for man. It is the *student's* day, whereon he may turn from the ordinary to the sublimer world of thought and find new inspiration for his daily endeavor. It is the *doubter's* day, on which he may investigate the most momentous questions of God and duty and destiny. It is the *children's* day, when the

The Universal Day

home circle may be perfect, and sweet memories be planted which shall fill the later years with their fragrance. The children need the gentle influence of the Sabbath. And if we who are no longer children were to give up ourselves to the consecration and the conservation of the day in the interest of the young life of the land, we should not only insure a better and a larger life to the next generation, but we should ourselves enter more fully and with greater plenitude of power into that kingdom of which its Founder said to his disciples, "Except ye be converted, and become as little children, ye shall not enter into the kingdom of God." The Sabbath is the *poor man's* day, when he can have leisure to reward the love of wife and children, go with them to the house of God, and enjoy to the full what Longfellow calls "the dear, delicious, silent Sunday, to the weary workman both of brain and hand the beloved day of rest." It is the *rich man's* day, when, if he will, he may throw off the burdens of anxiety and prove to his family that there are some

The Sabbath

things he prizes as much as stocks and estates and silver and gold—a day when he may transfer some of his treasures to the heavens and fix his heart on things above, where moth and rust cannot corrupt, nor thieves break through and steal. It is the *mourner's* day, on which eyes that weep in sore bereavement may look upward and hear a voice out of the heavens say, "In my Father's house are many mansions." It is the true *all saints'* day, when, rising above the littleness, the rivalries, the limitations of this life, we may look through Sabbath skies to the innumerable company in the city on Mount Zion, the heavenly Jerusalem, and sing:

"City of God, how broad and far outspread thy walls sublime!
The *true* thy chartered freemen are, of every age and clime.

"One holy church, one army strong, one steadfast high intent,
One working band, one harvest song, one King omnipotent!

"In vain the surges' angry shock, in vain the drifting sands;
Unharmed upon the eternal rock the eternal city stands."

The Day of Days

Therefore, as long as knowledge is better than ignorance, wisdom weightier than folly, righteousness worthier than sin, freedom better than bondage, earnestness nobler than frivolity, the whole people of greater value than a favored few, the soul more to be prized than the body, and eternity than time, let us prize highly, guard carefully, and keep holy the Sabbath day, the day of the Son of man, the day of the sons of God.

Immutability

By
M. Woolsey Stryker, D.D., LL.D.
President of Hamilton College, Clinton, N. Y.

"That those things which are not shaken may remain."
—Heb. xii. 27.

WERE the Bible less complimented and more appreciated it would be read far more naturally. It has no magical effect. Though it is *the* Book, it is a *book*, and a book whose natural history is part of its superlative value. Its origin was not artificial, and the special occasion and accent—the adaptation of each several part to a certain set of circumstances—give to each part its own peculiar value and explanation. We want the point of view, and what is called "introduction" is therefore indispensable. Who, e.g., were Timothy and Paul? what was

The Record of Process

Crete, Corinth? how did the Galatians differ from the Philippians? It is true of the Bible also, and because it is so august, *nascitur non fit*. The divine wisdom embodied in the very process and progress of revelation is one note of its authority—each strand is dyed in the colors of its own time. It is this normal variety that leads us to be sure of that supreme unity in which all the books are providential chapters of one persistent and ever-augmenting interpretation of the spirit of man learning to understand the inspiration of the Almighty. Just because this whole Book goes deepest into origins and ends, man's nature and God's nature, it is the most natural book in the world. We must never think that the supernatural is *extra*-natural. The Bible is not outside of human nature, but at its core. Nature is not shallow; it too is a book; and the Bible is a book supernaturally natural. It would be a great gain if all this collection of writings could be set in chronological sequence; the nearer we can come to such a mental arrangement of them

Immutability

the better for our comprehension. How shall you get the force of Ezra or Jeremiah or Amos if you do not know their dates? The historical anatomy of the Book underlies its physiology.

Of the twenty-seven New Testament books, one is a great prophetic prose poem, five are simple narratives, and twenty-one are letters. This last is the most flexible and the most personal form of writing. As it was the most natural method for the apostles to use, so its familiar facility best met the needs of those diverse persons and groups. Even its abstract paragraphs are always quick and warm. The whole New Testament is full of local color and is incident to actual life. This "touch of nature," this circumstantiality, this intense timeliness, sign it with the signature of an all-compassing Providence. Because so vital it is perennial. God's Spirit breathes through it.

Who reads a letter piecemeal? A letter is meant for one sitting and a whole impression. These twenty-one letters are to be felt in their individual completeness. "Who, when, where, why, what?" Notably does the letter to the Hebrews require and reward a careful search for its dominant thought and intent. It surely is among the six or seven books of the New Testament foremost in importance.

It has singular value as a book of *relations*—showing the fulfilment of the Old Testament spirit in the spirit of the New. A perfect commentary upon Leviticus, it declares the moral inviolability of God's one only covenant; it explains the merging of the dispensation of Israel in that of the Christian church, and the completion of all ritual and symbol in Him whom that system had prefigured and for whom it had prepared. It interprets every tradition and precedent as transfigured in Jesus the Christ, and while using the largest retrospect rebukes the idolatry which can only look back.

But though the letter is such an ample demonstration, it is more—an appeal. The general scope of the argument is made glowing hot by its special address to the trouble

Immutability

and anxiety of those to whom just then the problem of transition was of painful and all but overwhelming perplexity. Here lies the ardor, the pathos, the penetration of whoever he was that penned it. This cardinal adaptation to that time is what adapts it to all times of strangeness and misgiving. Bishop Westcott says (" C. C.," p. 4): " No men were ever called to endure greater sacrifices, to surrender more precious hopes, to bear deeper disappointments, than those to whom this epistle was first addressed"; and he opens its inmost secret in declaring that it was written *" to those who were undergoing the trials of a new age."* This is indeed its message—a perpetual lesson for all souls baffled and hesitating under the exactions and special apprehensions of a changing time.

From that Jewish Christian whom this letter takes by the hand how much that he held sacred seemed to be slipping away! How could he turn from that solemn and splendid past and all at once be adjusted to what seemed to disregard customs and associations

Fulfilment

intertwined with his deepest life? The Hebrew had and held in veneration a nation, a liturgy, a temple, and a law; how could he, without sharp travail, comprehend that there had been ushered in that which was larger than the nation, grander than the temple, more hallowed than the old ceremonial, deeper than the law; and that patriotism, worship, reverence, obedience, under new forms, were to be kept not only, but enlarged?

No wonder that some, startled and distressed, drew back from what seemed to them a collapse. No wonder that, unable so swiftly to distinguish between the transient and the permanent, some devout souls, caught in the throes of such a period, found faith itself in jeopardy. To show such how the chosen people was the vessel of a world redemption; how the chrysalis ages were surpassed; that Christ was not a destroyer, but a fulfiller, in whom all the ancient things had come to their consummation—this was the task of love the epistle so wondrously per-

Immutability

formed. Its whole motif and criterion is the evolution of an all-consistent, all-embracing purpose, which glorified the past, not as a sunsetting, but as a dawn. Your more deliberate reading may well analyze and array this great translation of Hebrew thought into Christian thought, but even the swift allusion (which is all our present limit allows) can give us the organ note that sounds the constant key. More than any other New Testament writing this compact letter is ruled by the method of comparison and antithesis. All its detail is organized under contrast. Every stroke declares that reëstablishment is the purpose of all disestablishment; that, whatever good God takes, he gives a better, leading on to the best; that where he supplants he replants. And the final appeal is to that affinity with him which disappoints all fears and teaches the heart to "hold fast the confession of hope, that it waver not." "The law but a shadow of good things to come"; "the disannulling of the commandment, and the bringing in of a better hope";

The Building More than its Scaffold

"a better covenant, enacted upon better promises"; "a greater and more perfect tabernacle"; "One worthy of more glory than Moses"; "a perpetual High Priest"; "a continuing city"; "a kingdom that cannot be shaken"; "He taketh away the first, that he may establish the second." These contrasts, and many more their like, declare the immanent, the perdurable, the immutable care of a God under whom they are not to "shrink back," but to *believe;* and at that word out blazes the sublime definition of xi. 1, and, the skies shriveling as in an amphitheater, whereof all ages are the spectators and each present age the spectacle, there is disclosed the "great cloud of witnesses," and there is declared that moral continuity of all believing generations in which the past is forever perfecting in the "better things" provided through each new present.

The culmination of the epistle lies in our text, but the full chord was struck in its opening phrase (i. 1): "*God*, who," etc.

Here lies the appeal to our hearts. By all

Immutability

this raptured argument the Faithful One challenges our confidence. Amid shaken circumstance unshaken Providence! Out of darkness the Shechinah! Through the shattering of forms, the displacement of custom, the overruling of precedents, over all and in all, *God!*

Here are the elements of all human discipline. Here is a solvent for the uncertainties and reluctancy of every age, unexpectant because too self-centered. God is the same, and "Jesus Christ is the same yesterday, and to-day, and forever." He "cannot deny himself," and still declares, "It is I; be not afraid." He leads all generations and leads each soul. To his fidelity we are to cleave rather than to our associations with his past method. In all swirl and gloom it is our experience of *him*, rather than any forecast of his *way*, that must steady us.

The secret of life is growth, prolonging its identity while ever weaving new garments. Our very bodies are a parable of the uses of change. Literally they "die daily." As in

Whatever Lives Moves

walking one perpetually loses and regains his balance, taking ground with the heel and leaving it with the toes, and thus moving, so advances the soul—every new foothold a new point of departure. Retrograde is not man's natural gait; it is the crab that creeps ahead and runs backward! As the oncoming buds of spring push off the leaves of autumn, so we doff the old summer and don the new. Life is more than its leaves, and so (" as the days of a tree "), " though the outward perishes, the inner is renewed day by day." This is the penalty and reward of our birthright. Immortal life must be perpetual motion. Biology transcends morphology and is a spiritual science. Whatever has come to a standstill is dead. Then it may be dissected, but not revived. The open secret of life is lost. That is kept elsewhere than in *disjecta membra;* it is at the other end of the knife.

Following neither the extremists, who retain all form, nor those who abandon all substance, and discerning between the abso-

Immutability

lute and the relative, we can avow, as did Jeremiah (xvii. 12) in other tumultuous and seismic days, "A glorious throne, set on high from the beginning, is the place of our sanctuary."

With such comfort to courage as the believing Hebrews of the first Christian century received this letter, so may we take it in this latest century, which cannot be the last. Each *annus Domini* must trace the past, not to repeat, but to surpass, still going on into the future's explorations with Him who never stops. The developing parts which fear calls fragments faith holds as portions, and finds their implication by not detaching and isolating them.

In "the first and the last and the living One" we live and move. This is the legibility of duty and the philosophy of history. What seems to indolence and timidity an emergency, or even a catastrophe, is but one clause of that revelation which is punctuated with commas and whose continuous sense uses no disjunctives and attains no period.

The Point of View

It is they who "have no changes" who fear not God. Eccentricity is dislocation. To him who stations himself upon what is central every enlarging circumference is normal. All new experience is serious, but to the reverent mind it is always precious in its recall to "the things that cannot be shaken." Our vicissitudes are kindly in setting aside secondary things and in putting forward what is primary, in turning us from the symbol to the sense, in bringing us back to our necessary selves. Dislodgments from ease and complacency (and from their neglects and torpors) invite us to where we can neither be disappointed nor surprised. "Emptied from vessel to vessel" and educated in expectant attention, we get by heart that old solace, "My soul, wait thou only upon God." If nothing is so disagreeable, so dreary, so futile, as religion without him, nothing is so deep and sure as he. Faithfulness to the "two immutable things" (his "word" and his "oath") can never know monotony or imagine danger. In the rapids

Immutability

it is certain of the helmsman. "At the core of the cyclone it finds a place of total calm."

> "Let us be like the bird, one instant lighted
> Upon a twig that swings;
> He feels it yield, but sings on unaffrighted,
> Knowing he has his wings."

As in a distant land the appearance of a dear friend can make strange scenes homelike, so the recognition of the constancy of God can surmount all the tremors of a lonely heart.

Or do we ponder the riddle of this our time—its incisive, insistent questions, its mental pace and strain? God has not forgotten. "Progress is made by shaking to its center all that is uncritical." So has every science been purged of guesses, and so shall still be. Our definitions and explanations are provisional. They are like the manna, "good for this day only." God is not peradventured upon our theodicies.

The great world's convulsions usher the kingdom that cannot be shaken. Not even the hideous disconcert of the so-called Christian powers can long bar back the Son of man. He will break their insolent bluster with a rod of iron.

Well may we go on with God and "nightly pitch a moving tent," though all we are sure of is "God"; that syllable is central. What if we stand in the fog, so we stand on that Rock?

"Bright shoots of everlastingnesse" already begin "the morning without clouds" which puzzled and troubled souls shall know whose very difficulties forced them to venture all upon Him "with whom there is no parallax or eclipse."

The Sinless One

By
George T. Purves, D.D.
Professor of New Testament Literature in Princeton Theological Seminary

"For such an high priest became us, who is holy, harmless, undefiled, separate from sinners." — *Heb. vii. 26.*

WHATEVER makes the person of Jesus Christ vividly real to our thoughts helps us in our daily lives. Practical Christianity finds a mighty stimulus in trusting contemplating, understanding, and following, him; for in so doing we learn to live with God and for man. He is the personal center of our religion, the living revelation of truth and life, the magnet by which we are drawn heavenward, the one in and by whom salvation becomes an actual possession. And yet thus vividly and truthfully to apprehend him is not easy. Being invisible he does not

stand so clearly before us as other objects which address themselves to our senses. The historical distance from us of his earthly career is apt to make his figure indistinct. Even our dogmatic conceptions of his person and work sometimes become formal and lifeless, though intended to interpret him and though correctly expressing what we should believe about him. It ought, therefore, to be our effort constantly to repaint his figure upon the canvas of our thought, to turn upon him the light of experience and research, of comparison and analysis, that fresh ideas of his unspeakable glory may daily dawn upon our minds, may delight our hearts, and cause us to give him all the admiration and devotion of which we may be capable.

Now in the words of our text we have briefly described the moral purity of Jesus, the sinless, unspotted excellence of his personal character. The language is very vivid. It shows the profound impression which Jesus made on the first generation of disciples—the immediate reflection of the impres-

The Sinless One

sion made on those who came into direct contact with him. The words breathe the realism of personal acquaintance. They do not enlarge upon what all knew, but they express very beautifully the sense of ineffable purity and holiness, of infinite moral superiority, which the disciples received from him whose very presence had revealed a new and heavenly life. He was "holy"; and the Greek word is not the common one for a thing set apart for sacred usage, but a word less often employed and indicative of an exquisitely pure and lofty character, one that realized and discharged all its obligations. He was "harmless," i.e., thoroughly good, gentle, benevolent, tender-hearted, and true. Out of him as they remembered him no harm ever proceeded. No evil ever issued from act or word of his. Nothing but good came from him. When we remember how much we influence one another, and how much evil goes forth even from the best of us to counterbalance not a little of the good we do, we shall appreciate the character of the One of

Spiritual Separation

whom it could be said by those who knew him best that he was, as he bade them to be, "harmless as a dove." Further, he was "undefiled"—untainted by the corruption of the world in which he dwelt, unspotted by the passions which left a stain even on apostles. In short, he was "separate from sinners." Some would take these words with those that follow, "made higher than the heavens," and understand them to describe our Lord as now separated at the right hand of God from the world of sinners, even as the high priest in the most holy place was separated from the multitude for whom he made atonement. But I judge it more natural to see in the words another phrase to describe Christ's personal character. He was separated from sinners. The disciples who stood nearest to him felt that there was a great chasm between his spotless soul and theirs. He was on a plane above them. His motives and purposes were unlike theirs. And this although in other respects he was so near to them and so truly man. He had

The Sinless One

laid hold, as this epistle says, on the seed of Abraham. He was touched with the feeling of their infirmities. He was full of sympathy and friendship. He understood them. He took them by the hand. He wept over their griefs and rejoiced in their joys. Yet he was evidently as far above them as the gleaming stars were higher than the water in which their brilliance was reflected. He was the friend of publicans and harlots, and yet he was "separate from sinners."

Could any language more forcibly express the sense which the disciples had of their Master's sinlessness? As I have said, the words indicate the realism of personal acquaintance. They do not speak in the language of the schools. They do not measure Christ's worth by formal standards. They are the outcome of personal adoration and unspeakable reverence for One whose character and life had been to those who knew him the disclosure of the absolutely good.

Now I desire to enable you, if possible, to realize afresh the sinlessness of Jesus Christ

No Sense of Sin

by suggesting certain considerations which ought to make it very clear and very astonishing to our minds. I would exalt your sense of his personal perfection,—unlike that of any other character who has ever appeared in the history of our race,—and I would do it, not by a formal proof of the doctrine, but by setting his life in its surroundings, with the hope that the same impression may be made on our minds as on those who knew him first.

1. Consider, then, that in all the records which we have of the Lord Jesus there is not the slightest betrayal by him of the least degree of the consciousness of sin. We have a sufficiently complete record to justify us in saying that this is a fact. We see him in most trying hours. We hear him pray. We listen to his teaching on religious themes. We hear him reprove others. We catch glimpses of him in private as well as in public. We know that he spake often about himself. But in all the life of Christ we never hear any confession of unworthiness or

The Sinless One

any longing after holiness, or discover any indication whatever that he felt himself in the least degree touched by sin.

The significance of this will appear if we recall two other facts, one of experience, the other of history.

The first is that, as a matter of universal experience, the more spiritual a man becomes the more does he feel himself a sinner and unworthy of fellowship with God. The progress of man's moral life commonly consists in the awakening and sharpening of his conscience. He becomes more keenly aware of moral obligations. He sees them where before he saw them not. He analyzes more thoroughly his motives and classifies more correctly his duties. He becomes more sensitive to the demands made upon his conscience, just as progress in other departments of activity consists in the refinement of our powers and the larger perception of the objects on which they were meant to terminate. This is the law of the moral and spiritual life of man. He is at first a child, and, like a

The Growth of Conscience

child, only takes in a few facts, feels his obligations in but a few directions. Some men never grow beyond this stage. Though their intellects may be cultured and their bodies strengthened, their moral faculties remain undeveloped. Then conscience is apt to become a mere scourge, driving to unloved duty; a nightmare, affrighting with threats of torment. But just so far as the spiritual life of man has blossomed and flowered, so far has his sensitiveness to evil increased, his recognition of it brightened and clarified, his consciousness of its presence in him become more intense, and his longings after freedom from it become stronger. Witness in proof of this the hymns of all religions, and especially the hymns of Christendom. Witness the advance of social morality, taking in, as it has gradually done, matters that were once thought quite indifferent. Read the confessions of the purest men and women who have ever lived. Those that have risen highest have felt themselves the lowest. And this has not been a delusion with them; they

The Sinless One

have only seen more clearly. A villainous murderer went to the scaffold saying that he looked on his life as a whole with much satisfaction, and felt that, with the trifling exception of a murder, he had tried to do right by all men. Augustine wrote, "The dwelling of my soul is in ruins; do Thou restore it. There is that in it which must offend thine eyes; I confess and know it: but who will cleanse it?" Such are fair examples. Who of us that try to love God does not know the same thing from his own experience? As Christian life proceeds, as its insight becomes clearer, as its consciousness deepens and is purified, it becomes more and more ready to say with the Scripture, "In my flesh there dwelleth no good thing," and to repeat confessions at which the world sometimes stands amazed. Just in proportion as man's moral life advances does he feel that he is not worthy even to gather up the crumbs that fall from the festal table which the grace of God has spread.

But lo! the one person who by act and

The Call to Repentance

word gave evidence of the most spiritual life was absolutely without this element of mind. He had the clearest insight into moral duties. His words are still recognized as embodying the loftiest ethics. His character is held worthy of universal imitation. He loved to pray. He talked with God as though he saw him. And yet, unlike every other man of spiritual insight who ever lived, he never betrayed any sense of unworthiness or of his need of greater holiness.

And this stands out still more remarkably when we associate it with the historical fact that in the Jewish world in which Jesus lived the sense of sin and of general apostasy from God was specially strong among awakened minds. Jesus lived in the age when John cried to all Israel "Repent!" and with prophetic zeal unveiled the monstrous corruption of the church and nation. But John himself very plainly confessed his own unworthiness. Speaking of Messiah, he said, "His shoe's latchet I am not worthy to unloose." So, likewise, those men who followed

The Sinless One

Jesus were very emphatic in their confessions of sin. Peter cried, "I am a sinful man, O Lord." The centurion said, "I am not worthy that thou shouldest come under my roof." Paul called himself "the chief of sinners." Wherever Christ or his gospel went men were awakened in an eminent degree to the fact of sin, and were led to confess that, even if believers, they were only beginning to aspire to that holiness without which they felt that no man can see the Lord.

But again, amid this whole movement and as the vital center of it, the Lord Jesus never betrayed the slightest consciousness of wrong. If he had been the product of the same influences which molded the rest, he would have been the loudest in his confessions. But not an accent of such fell from his lips. How does the consciousness of sin show itself? With some in fear, causing them to turn away from God and dread to think of him, much more to pray. With others it assumes the form of bravado, leading them to boldly dare the consequences of their mis-

No Need of Forgiveness

deeds. These effects, however, are seen in characters which cannot possibly be compared with Christ's. With good men, on the other hand, who have been awakened to a sense of sin, it shows itself in expressions of repentance, in prayers for forgiveness, in longings after holiness, in acknowledgment of the unmerited grace of God; sometimes in painful acts of self-denial and asceticism, which are supposed to compensate for transgression or to extinguish the power of evil. But none of these things are discoverable in Jesus. Though he called others to repent, he himself never expressed repentance. He never asked to be forgiven, though he taught us to ask it. On the contrary, we find him rejoicing in the assurance of his Father's eternal love, delighting in communion with God, and finally openly challenging his enemies on this very point: "Which of you convinceth me of sin?" Nor is there any trace of development in his spiritual life, but, from the first and to the last, the utter absence of the consciousness of sin appears in him. The

The Sinless One

Buddha claimed to reach perfection, but only as the result of a long and painful process of self-purification. Christ appears as free from the sense of sin in the beginning of his career as amid its close.

Is not this a life which stands alone in all history? Try to imagine if it be possible on the ordinary suppositions of human experience. How could one be gifted with such spiritual discernment and yet see no flaw in himself, if there was a flaw? How could one teach such high and pure morals without confessing his own shortcomings, if he did come short? How could one dwell so near to the divine Father and never ask to be forgiven sin, which that Father hates, if there was any sin to be forgiven? I ask you to think of this, not from the standpoint of the deity of Christ in which we believe, but from the standpoint of his humanity. Conceive the impression which he must have made upon those about him. Realize that he was an actual living person. Then you will appreciate the fact that in all the record of his

Credibility of the Gospels

life there is not a trace of the slightest sense of sin. "If I should say, I know not the Father," said Jesus to the Pharisees, "I should be a liar like unto you: but I know him, and keep his sayings." "I do always those things which please him." Such expressions, embedded in such a life, form a unique fact in the history of moral teaching.

2. There are only two ways by which those who doubt these facts can evade the force of the evidence. The first is by saying that the record in the gospels is not true, but that the disciples exaggerated the character of their Master, embellished his virtues and forgot his faults. To reply to this objection would lead us too far afield. It involves the whole question of the credibility of the gospels. But I may point out in passing that the gospels do describe Christ's weakness and weariness, his struggles with temptation and his agony in the garden. They evince no disposition, therefore, to idealize the character of Jesus, nor to hide his genuine humanity. On the other hand, they do not, except

in the prologue to the fourth gospel, bring out the formal doctrine about him which the apostles themselves believed, nor do they impute to the Master the theological language which later revelations would have justified. They have therefore all the appearance of honest histories. They confirm one another. They are themselves confirmed by the epistles. The very simplicity of their story attests their historical veracity.

The other way to escape the natural inference from the facts of which we have been speaking is to say that Jesus was under an hallucination, that his enthusiasm made him blind to his own defects. So Renan writes: "Jesus cannot be judged by the rule of our petty propriety. The admiration of his disciples overwhelmed him and carried him away."

I wish, therefore, to suggest certain other facts which render these objections highly improbable, and which also serve to give a still livelier sense of the real sinlessness of our Lord.

The Disciples' Testimony

The first is that it was those who were nearest to him who have testified to his spotless purity. It is quite easy to make a good impression on the public. It is not so easy to extort from those who live with us a similar tribute, unless it be deserved. Many men seem great and good at a distance, but nearer at hand their faults are manifest. Now the fact was that in public Jesus was often charged with doing wrong. The Pharisees openly called him a sinner because they thought he broke the Sabbath, and a devil because he opposed them, and a blasphemer because he said God was his Father. He did not live such a life as to be called a saint by the established standard of the day. His reputation was not based on conformity to the common ideal. On the contrary, he was crucified as a malefactor. It was only those who lived with him who testify to the spotless beauty of his character. They saw him in private. They watched him in his most critical hours. They heard his ejaculations. They were his confidential friends. But it was they who from the very first acknowledged, and with greater emphasis as their acquaintance with him ripened, that he was the Holy One of God. Their testimony seems of great worth. Popular applause is easy to win if we conform to the popular ideal, but this testimony was rendered, in the face of derision and apparent failure, by those who knew him best.

Furthermore, nothing that Jesus ever said or did appears even now to indicate sin in him. We have grown very wise. Some think that, speaking comparatively, we have grown good. Certainly the world has greatly advanced in the knowledge of duty. But it is a fact that we cannot find anything to criticize in Jesus from a moral point of view. All that we can do, whether Christians or not, from theologians to novelists, is to show that our teachings were his. He can still say, "Which of you convinceth me of sin?" In this age, for example, we lay great stress on the love of man as the highest form of morality; on benevolence, unselfishness, on

Sinless though Tempted

altruism. But all this was taught and practised ages ago by Jesus. Or, if we say that morality depends on the motives from which men act, what motives can be higher than those which appear in the life of Jesus? The Sermon on the Mount is the moral code of the ages, and point, if you can, to any principle or precept of that sermon which Jesus did not obey in his life. I need not expand on this; but I beg you to remember that the growing moral sense of nineteen centuries has not convicted him of any fault of character.

And still again, remember that he made this impression on his friends and gave this evidence in his life although he was perfectly open to temptation and, in fact, fought it hand to hand. He was not a cold ideal. He was not a statue in marble. Life's battle was tremendously real to him. He was tempted as we are. He grew also in knowledge and wisdom. And therefore the spotless holiness of his character becomes of treble worth. It appears a living attainment.

The Sinless One

It was a conquest. It was a thoroughly human quality, and must on that account have impressed the more those who were about him. We need not stumble over the notion that a sinless person cannot be tempted. If our first parents were tempted and fell, Christ could be tempted without falling. Moreover, the power of temptation consists simply in its offering us something that we desire; and Jesus desired much that he could not have, if he were to become man's Redeemer. It was his lot to lay aside the enjoyment of Heaven's favor; to apparently fail of winning men to God; at last to have the Father hide his face from him. His temptations lay in the desire for these good things which were forbidden him, and the very intensity of his love of God and man made the temptations stronger. At any rate the testimony is unanimous that he knew temptation's power. The battle in the wilderness of Judea, the agony in the garden of Gethsemane, the remark that fell from his lips, "I have overcome the world," sufficiently

What is Sin?

attest it. This very writer of the Epistle to the Hebrews knew it. He says, "He was in all points tempted like as we are, yet without sin." "In that he himself hath suffered being tempted, he is able to succor them that are tempted." The disciples knew him too well to claim for him exemption from the common lot. They saw him harassed and oppressed, and therefore bowed the more reverently before the meekness and gentleness, the purity and love, the unselfishness and the righteousness which in spite of temptation never failed to manifest themselves in Jesus. This adds immensely to our admiration of his character. He is one of ourselves. The holiness of God may be too far above us for us to comprehend it, but the spotless purity of the tempted Saviour, who will not adore?

And now, once more, I add that the Lord Jesus had for his confessed rule of life a principle which naturally made him realize keenly the presence of sin, even in its least apparent forms. He said, "My meat is to do the will of him that sent me"; and through all his

The Sinless One

life the will of God was his law, to do that will was his firm resolve. I ask you to note this particularly; for a man's sense of sin depends directly upon his idea of what sin is. Many people think that only crime is sin, and because they have done no crime they feel no sense of sin. Others think sin to be merely selfishness, and because they are kind and philanthropic do not regard themselves as seriously at fault. But the Bible teaches that sin is far more than this. It is any want of conformity to the will of God. Man owes to God absolute loyalty of thought and act. The least rupture of that loyalty is sin. The broader and deeper our knowledge of the will of God, the more must we feel that we are sinful. Now my point is that Jesus was fully aware of this. This was his rule; by this he judged. And he gives evidence of so broad and deep a knowledge of what God's will is that the rule of his life made him sensible of sin to a degree in comparison with which our best perceptions of it are as twilight to high noon. And yet he had no sense of sin.

Christ's Credentials

Though he had the highest possible standard by which to judge, he never felt that the standard condemned him. Though he was keenly alive to moral differences, though he stands before us the supreme Teacher of what is right, though he had for his rule of life the highest of all laws, he deliberately said, " I have overcome the world "; " I have finished the work which thou gavest me to do."

Fellow-sinners, what a character is this! It defies all explanations save that of the text. A man, yet a sinless man! Tempted, but never stained! Fighting hand to hand with evil, but never wounded by it! In the world, and yet above it! Once and only once in human history has this spectacle appeared.

Permit me, then, in a word, to press upon your minds the practical importance of this truth.

The moral character of Jesus is a sufficient credential of the truth of his gospel. He has other credentials, but I bring forward this to-day. He is unique. He is truth and righteousness incarnate. Therefore his word must

The Sinless One

be authoritative; his teaching concerning God and duty, truth and salvation, must be our absolute standard. He guarantees by his personal sinlessness the authority of the message. What he declares to be God's truth we must accept as such. What he declares to be God's will and purpose we must obey and believe. We scarcely need other evidence. At his feet mind and heart should bow.

Further, he is worthy to be man's representative before God. Sinless himself, he is a rightful priest of humanity. So our text says, "Such an high priest became us." This is what we need. Who but he can venture for us into the most holy place? Who but he can sprinkle the atoning blood? He is a priest whose right to mediate history and conscience, as well as God, declare.

For can we suppose that this sinless life was lived for himself alone? He himself assures us of the contrary. He came into the world. He did not belong to it. He had no need to live on earth at all. His express

Our Great High Priest

declaration is that he came for our redemption. If so, we must certainly behold in his sinless life more even than the perfect example of what our lives should be. It was the necessary preparation for the sacrifice of the cross, and it becomes more than ever precious when we consider that it was part of the redemption price paid for our deliverance. For we are "not redeemed with corruptible things, as silver and gold, but with the precious blood of Christ, as of a Lamb without blemish and without spot." The character which the world itself cannot but admire, and the life which stands forth as the great exception to all other lives, obtain the highest significance when we also remember that God "hath made him to be sin for us, who knew no sin; that we might be made the righteousness of God in him." Well may we adore him. Well may we imitate and obey him. But above all else, well may we trust him; for he has won the right to redeem us, and is able to save unto the uttermost all those that come unto God by him.